WHEN LIFE IS CHANGED FOREVER

RICK TAYLOR

HARVEST HOUSE PUBLISHERS
Eugene, Oregon 97402

WHEN LIFE IS CHANGED FOREVER

Copyright © 1992 by Harvest House Publishers
Eugene, Oregon 97402

Taylor, Patrick, 1948—
    When life is changed forever : by the death of someone near / Patrick Taylor.
        p. cm.
    Includes bibliographical references.
    ISBN 0-89081-971-8
    1. Death—Religious aspects—Christianity. 2. Taylor, Patrick, 1948– .
I. Title.
BT825.T36   1993   93-4836
248.8′6—dc20   CIP

This book is lovingly dedicated to

my wife, Judy, and our four children:
Kyle, Bryan, Eric, and Kelly.

They have each taught me so much
about life and living
. . . even in the midst of death.

CONTENTS

ACKNOWLEDGEMENTS

I would like to express my sincere appreciation to:

Eileen Mason and *Bob Hawkins, Jr.*, for believing I had something to say that could truly help other people;

Betty Fletcher, who, through her editing skills, helped me say it;

Bob Welch, a friend who kept encouraging me in the process;

The whole congregation of *Grace Community Fellowship*, who continually give me the freedom and the exhortation to keep growing and stretching; and

Dr. Lanier Burns, for challenging me to undertake and follow through on this endeavor.

A
Personal Note
from the Author

There was a time when my only thoughts about death revolved around my own dying. In most ways I felt prepared for death and eternity, but in a moment of time I was confronted with the reality that I was not nearly so prepared for *life*... life after the loss of a loved one.

Losing someone I loved was an experience that wounded me deeply. My emotions and my mind flared from sadness and dismay to fierce anger and doubt. The world of my heart was turned upside down, and the passing of time did not seem to heal the wound left by death's visit.

Life became a struggle to get back to "normal." It took many months, even years, before I began to realize that normal, whatever it was, had been permanently altered. Part of what had made my life what it was had been torn away, never to return. Only then did I realize that God, my loving Father, wanted to use this tragedy, though He hated it, to change me into more of the person He had designed me to be.

It has always been my deep desire that this book not be about me, though the story of my loss is woven throughout these pages. I share my family's story only to help you come to grips with what you must be feeling and the questions that you must be asking, and to help you make choices that will better enable you to experience God's "promise of life" (2 Timothy 1:1), beginning right now. This book is not simply about death; it is about life. I trust God to use these words to help you experience His fullness of life... even in the midst of your pain and sorrow.

—Rick Taylor

Feeling Death

---

*When one is bereaved, one feels out of touch
with the mainstream, different, unable to
connect. One feels stigmatized, deprived,
and angry for being selected to suffer.*

—Joan Hagen Arnold and
Penelope Buschman Gemma

Chapter 1

A Bright Beginning

Lord, you have assigned me my portion and my cup;
*   you have made my lot secure.*
The boundary lines have fallen for me in pleasant places;
*   surely I have a delightful inheritance.*

✦ Psalm 16:5,6

IT HAD BEEN A LONG DAY. Wearily I sank onto the couch and into the secluded world of my own thoughts. Suddenly I was attacked by three small boys who didn't care a bit about my hard day. Their rough-and-tumble, knees-in-the-stomach attitude had a way of propelling me from my world of self-reflection to the arena of floor wrestling. Their yells and screams of laughter, "Daddy, stop!" and "Daddy, I'm getting the hiccups" filled our small mobile home. I knew they didn't mean a word of it. This was exactly what they wanted from their dad right now.

Then just as suddenly they were off again, onto their next rampaging adventure. "Thank you, God," I thought, "for giving me such bundles of joy and laughter!" With that thought I slipped into the kitchen, looking for the mischievous mother of those little rascals. I knew she was behind the sneak-attack I had just survived. She had trained our sons with a variety of commands such as "Come on, guys, Dad's home!" or "Boys, Dad's on the couch alone."

Stealing up behind her, I gave her a gentle poke in the ribs. As she jumped and turned I pulled her very close and kissed her. Then I whispered in her ear, "You deserved that!" She hit me with her potholder, but the twinkle in her eyes was a clear admission of guilt. Having taken my revenge, I walked back to my couch of reflection with a heart full of gratitude.

How could one man be so blessed? As I looked at our family in the early spring of 1979, I knew we had the kind of home that makes for "happily ever after" stories.

After pastoring a busy Florida church for a number of years, I had recently taken the opportunity to become a director of a Christian camp, Pine Cove Conference Center, where Judy and I had met and fallen in love ten years earlier. With three young sons growing all too quickly, we believed it would please the Lord for us to spend more time together as a family, building for the future.

God had given Judy and me a strong marriage and a loving friendship. Our hectic pastoral schedule had left us weary, but our love and commitment kept mending the frayed edges in our lives. The country setting with horses, room to run, and opportunities for family life was just what we had needed.

We basked in the joy of raising our three stair-stepped boys: Kyle, our firstborn, who was 5½, Bryan, 3½, and Eric, 2½. Each was unique and completely wonderful to us.

Kyle was the leader of the pack—and all too often the ringleader. Bright and energetic, Kyle had a voracious appetite for living and learning. At age two he shocked us when he walked over to our set of encyclopedias and, pointing to each letter, went through the alphabet. When he turned five he began attending a private school where he was excelling, especially in French, reading, and music.

One day a friend of ours thanked Judy for letting Kyle carpool with her. On the way back and forth to school they shared deep discussions about life and God. Just that day they had passed a dog that had been killed and left lying on the side of the country road. Kyle had initiated a lengthy conversation about death, and life after death, for dogs and people.

At home Kyle assumed he was in charge, the ever-on-duty oldest child. The other two boys were "his" brothers, and he was their self-appointed mentor. I can't remember how many times I had to remind Kyle that I was the dad. He would tell Bryan and Eric when to get up, what to play, and when to brush their teeth. If we let him, he would even tell his brothers, who slept in the same small room, when to go to sleep. At night he would sing and pray to Jesus with such fervor that it drove Judy and me to our knees. He was a constant surprise and joy to us.

Bryan was two years younger than Kyle. He had a contagious laugh and could eat us all under the table, especially when it came to ice cream. But because Kyle was so domineering, Bryan had little choice those first few years but to be the chief follower to his big brother. Bryan looked to Kyle for advice on all facets of life as a three-year-old.

Although he was quiet, Bryan was as tough as nails. He would hit his head hard, get up and rub the forming knot, and then take off for more action. As strong as an ox, Bryan could keep up with his older brother in almost everything except talking. None of us could do that!

Eric was 14 months younger than Bryan, and from day one he was his own person. He was an independent boy, and even Kyle struggled with this little person who refused to be anything but who he himself decided to be. Though younger than his brothers, Eric was determined to keep up with them both and wasn't afraid to voice his opinions forcefully, letting volume make up for vocabulary.

It must have been a joy to be a child in the Taylor household. Judy made each day an adventure as she

relished being the total mom to our inquisitive and energetic brood. Their unending questions, childish spats,
and boundless enthusiasm kept her on the run. She
could see their potential bursting out all over—in their
dancing eyes and impish smiles, in their quick wit and
innocent wisdom, in their tears of sorrow and their
outbursts of unquenchable laughter.

Judy made the most of life as a camp director's wife.
She took the boys on walks in autumn to gather colored
leaves, then helped them create miniature masterpieces
with their colorful treasures. She took them on boat and
canoe rides, swimming in the pool, horseback riding,
and on adventure discovery walks in the cool of the
mornings.

And I was the proud and thankful dad to our sons.
What could be better than teaching three lovable boys to
throw and bat and catch and run and sing and laugh and
live? Each day was a miracle of discovery. Our little
family of five, with one on the way, was blessed by God
indeed. Who could ask for anything more?

Having spent a pleasant evening with these thoughts,
Judy and I finally turned out the lights and went to bed.

✦ ✦ ✦

"Kyle, stop singing and go to sleep!"

Just Another Day

The following morning began much like any other day
during the early spring in east Texas. The sky was gray
and clouded. Rain was sputtering off and on. It was brisk
in those early hours when Judy and I awoke. We lay in
bed, her head pillowed on my shoulder, talking quietly.
It was pure joy to share life with such a tender companion. We let time slip by, and then had to jump up and
tumble our three boys out of their beds so that we could

hurry to the main dining hall, about a mile away, to help prepare breakfast for the hundred or so guests in the lodge. Another Saturday morning had begun for the Taylor family.

The boys' beds were warm, and the floor of our house trailer was cold, so our efforts to hurry them up and out met with some resistance. But within a few minutes Kyle, Bryan, and Eric popped up and rolled into action. The engine of our happy family began to shift into high gear.

We all chattered busily as I warmed our van. The boys' shivering lips soon turned to smiles as they launched into short quips followed by bursts of sunny, contagious laughter.

We arrived in good time and began the ritual of trekking back and forth from the kitchen to the tables with dishes, napkins, and food. Soon the campers began their early morning migration into the dining hall, eager for a hearty breakfast and another day of fun and fellowship. After finishing our meal together, I reminded Judy that I needed to meet with Carl, our junior camp director, to go over the details of an upcoming camp. On my way out the door, I noticed Kyle walking toward the kitchen with a huge carton of milk in his arms. "Bye, Kyle," I called out. "I'll see you at lunch."

"Bye, Dad," came his reply. "I love you." His tender words warmed my heart. Lately he'd begun taking the initiative to tell me he loved me.

"What a special son!" my heart cheered as I closed the dining hall door.

The Shocking Announcement

About an hour later Carl and I wrapped up our camp planning at the maintenance building. We were good friends, and we enjoyed the leisurely walk back to my office. I knew that by now Judy and the boys were well on their way to town. One of Kyle's friends was having a birthday party, and all three boys were excited by the prospect of spending the morning with their playmates.

Suddenly through the gaps in the trees ahead of me I saw our van racing down the winding road toward my office. My thoughts went wild. *Judy doesn't drive that fast! She shouldn't be here. She should be in town by now. Oh, Lord, what's wrong?* My pace quickened. I could hear my heart beating wildly in my chest. I ran to the back of my office where she was headed. I was in full sprint as the van slid to a stop in the graveled parking lot. Judy, panic in her eyes, frantically rolled down the window.

"Get in quick! Kyle is dead and Eric is dying!" I could see Eric's pale, cold body in her arms. I jerked open the door and leaped into the driver's seat as Judy struggled to shift Eric's limp form to the passenger's seat with her. Bryan was in the back seat, teary eyed and very quiet. Judy tried to explain what had happened, but time was short. "We've got to get Eric to the hospital," I yelled, frantic to be on the way. I screamed at Carl to hurry to our place and find Kyle.

As I attacked the 13 miles of winding roads between camp and town, I took darting glances at Eric, lying limp in Judy's arms. He was blue and wet and dirty ... and horribly still. His eyes were rolled back, and only an occasional short gasp of air escaped his lips. Was the Eric I knew still in there? Where was the gleam in his eyes? Where was his smile? *Oh, God, I hate this. This can't be happening! Not to us!*

A million words hung in the eternal silence of that drive. Time stood still. Judy kept looking at Eric, her mother's arms holding him tightly, trying to keep the last bit of life from escaping. The pain etched on her face was indescribable.

As I drove to the hospital, Judy's announcement began to haunt the depths of my soul. "Kyle is dead. Eric is dying." The refrain repeated itself, over and over.

Something in my sunken heart broke. Such words had no place in our happy home. No father should have to hear them. No mother should have to utter them. Watching Eric, too weak to fight for his own life, made me desperate to keep death from taking two of my precious sons.

I did not know much about death at the time, but one thing was very clear to me—I hated it.

CHAPTER 2

The Unfolding Tragedy

My God, my God, why have you forsaken me?
Why are you so far from saving me,
so far from the words of my groaning?

✦ Psalm 22:1

IT WAS MONTHS BEFORE I knew all the horrors of that Saturday morning. I retreated from anyone who wanted to tell me the details of Kyle's terrible death. I didn't run away—yet in my own way I did. Judy had a deep need to talk about what happened. She had lived through a nightmare she had not asked for, but could not escape, and expressing her feelings helped. But I did not want to listen.

The children, too, were more than willing to talk about it. They reenacted the whole event almost daily. But I couldn't bear to watch. I didn't want to know.

So I hid in my work, 70 to 80 hours each week. And when I wasn't working, I escaped to the busyness of building our new home or into the refuge of having a new baby, Kelly, who needed my attention.

For nearly half a year I wrestled with God and my feelings. Finally I stopped and began to listen to Judy and the children. Slowly the pieces of the puzzle began to come together, and I realized the full terror of that cool and misty morning in April.

Judy and the boys had returned home from the dining hall to rewrap the present that one of the boys had "mistakenly" opened the night before. When they arrived at our tree-nestled home, the boys asked if they could go get their trikes, which they had left about a hundred feet from the house. "Okay," Judy replied, "but come right back. We don't want to be late." She needed a few minutes to rewrap the present anyway.

The boys took off down the path toward their trikes. As Bryan remembers, after they had retrieved their transportation Kyle suggested that they ride further down the path and around the pond, which was about the size of a baseball diamond.

"No," Bryan said. "That's too dangerous. The bikes might fall in."

"Well, then, let's walk around holding hands," Kyle urged. Still hesitant, but excited by the possibility of such an adventure, Bryan and Eric gave in to their older brother's idea . . . an idea that was completely foreign to our responsible oldest son since the boys were strictly forbidden to play by the water. About a third of the way around the pond was a small concrete spillway that regulated the level of water in the pond. During the rainy season we removed the board in the spillway so water could flow through, leaving a gap about 6" deep and 30" wide. Our three boys began to maneuver across the opening very carefully, one at a time. Kyle, with his longer legs, stepped across the span in the dam. Bryan managed to jump. But Eric's legs were too short, and in an instant he fell and rolled down into the water.

"Go get Mom!" Kyle yelled to Bryan. "I'm gonna get Eric."

"But you shouldn't go into the water," complained Bryan.

Kyle yelled back, "I have to. I have to save Eric. You go get Mom." With that he jumped in. Kyle paddled out to Eric, who was yelling and gasping for air. By the time Kyle reached him near the middle of the pond, Eric was still and lifeless. Kyle grabbed him and tried to pull him toward shore. "Bryan, I said go get Mom! Hurry! He's too heavy!"

Bryan started toward the house, but glanced back just long enough to see both of his brothers go under the water completely. The murky, bowl-shaped pond was perfectly still.

By this time Judy was desperately trying to find the boys. As she hurried toward where they were supposed to be, she heard loud crying. Sensing that something was desperately wrong, she ran in the direction of Bryan's uncontrollable sobs.

"Bryan," she cried. "What's wrong? Where are your brothers?"

"They're dying in the water," came his short, stabbing reply.

"Where in the water?" Judy frantically questioned. But Bryan was crying so hard he was unable to answer. Judy hurried with him to the pond, wanting to hold Bryan and comfort him, but feverishly needing to save her other two sons.

When they arrived the water was deathly calm. In terror, Judy began to wade out into the pond. Eight months pregnant and wearing shoes and long pants, she soon became stuck in the mire on the bottom. Seeing his mother up to her chest in the dark water, Bryan began to scream feverishly. Judy seized some long grass protruding from the bank.

Realizing the trauma Bryan was experiencing, Judy spoke to him quietly, calmly reassuring him that she was going to be okay. She again told him how important it was for him to try to remember where his brothers went into the water. After finally pulling herself out of the muddy water's edge, she began to maneuver around the pond, looking for signs of her sons. As she eased toward the spillway area where Bryan seemed to be leading her, her eyes kept searching for anything that might give her a clue to the whereabouts of her two precious boys.

"Please don't take two!" Judy pleaded, looking up toward the gray sky. Immediately she noticed the chest of one of the boys break the surface of the water. She dove in, pulled Eric onto the shore, and began trying to revive him. In that instant Judy felt a direct answer to her prayer. She somehow knew that she was seeing God's miraculous hand at work.

Her CPR training kicked into high gear and took over her every action and reaction. Between each breath into Eric's lifeless body, Judy was trying to calm and reassure Bryan, while at the same time scanning the surface of the pond to see if Kyle—the one who had taught her how to be a mom, who never seemed to mind that she had to learn everything from him first—was coming back, too.

After what seemed to Judy a lifetime of pushing and pounding and blowing into his ashen body, Eric finally gave a feeble gasp. Judy quickly rolled him onto his side, where he coughed up a lakeful of water. He immediately went into shock. Though his breaths were very shallow and weak, he *was* breathing and his heart was beating. With each breath, Judy was witnessing a miracle.

The Choice

At that instant Judy faced the hardest decision of her life. Should she stay and look for Kyle or get Eric to an emergency room immediately? As Eric began to breathe, Judy knew she had to leave Kyle, her flesh and blood, in that dark and lonely coffin of water. Kyle was gone. Judy's heart was broken that day, never to fully recover. Who could ever be the same after having to make such a choice?

Just then, Brad, an 18-year-old who lived in the mobile home next to us, came out to the pond. "Judy, is everything okay? I heard you yelling," he called to her. After telling him what had happened, Judy asked Brad to get a pole and try to get Kyle out of the water. Brad tried to convince her that Kyle was elsewhere...probably fallen, maybe a broken leg or arm, but not dead in that murky water. But Judy knew the truth. She told Brad to do as she said; she had to get to the hospital with Eric. With that she said goodbye to our firstborn son.

Judy wrested Eric from the muddy bank and, tugging at Bryan, ran to our van. At the hospital, the doctors and nurses scrambled to keep Eric from slipping away from us. Eric was in deep shock, his chilled body racked by uncontrollable shaking. The hospital staff fought to calm and warm him. About an hour later we were told that he had experienced a cold-water drowning. Because his lungs had been filled with the bacteria-ridden pond water, he would soon go into advanced pneumonia and it was very likely that he would die in his severely weakened condition.

Eric was alive, but far from stable. If he survived, the doctors did not know whether he would be the same sharp, quick-witted boy who had fallen into the pond. "Twenty-four hours will tell us a lot," they announced. They did not offer us much hope.

With puddles dripping from her wet clothes, Judy began telling one doctor that he did not understand. She had not witnessed one miracle already only to see Eric die. The doctor tried to comfort Judy but reaffirmed the likelihood that Eric would either die in the next few hours or suffer permanent brain damage.

The End of the Beginning

Our numb, grief-stricken family, minus one, held vigil that day and night in the hospital, watching for signs of life in Eric, and replaying the death of Kyle in our minds.

Judy was afraid that she might have hurt the baby inside her by diving into the cold pond and swallowing so much dirty, chemically treated water. The doctors shared her concern and felt that the stress might also have caused difficulties with the fetus. So we sat and waited for results from Eric's and Judy's X-rays, wondering if we might lose not only one, but two or even three of God's precious gifts to us.

Throughout the day and night a stream of friends came to the hospital. "How are you doing?" they asked, wanting to comfort us but not knowing how. I asked one friend to take care of the burial arrangements and another to try to keep our son's death from becoming a local media event. Yet another friend volunteered to go to the store to get diapers for Eric. It meant the world to have such special friends with us.

In the middle of the afternoon, some close friends from Florida, the Bentzels, called us in the hospital room. We had completely forgotten they were coming to spend part of their vacation with our family. They had called the camp and had been told only that we were at the hospital with the boys. Naturally they assumed that one of the boys had broken an arm or leg. It was unbelievably hard to hear Tom's typically jovial voice innocently joking, "What did those boys do now?"

I was at a total loss for words. The silence on my end of the phone was Tom's first clue that this might be much more than a skinned arm or leg. "Tom, Kyle is dead. And we are not sure if Eric is going to live." The silence on Tom's end of the phone was deafening. Then I heard Tom's sobbing voice as he told his family my announcement. Our conversation lasted only a moment at that point. Tom simply said they would be there as soon as they could. His broken, tearful voice echoed in my ears for hours that afternoon.

In the early evening our friend and physician, Dr. Knarr, came by to see Eric and us. He checked Eric and confirmed the prognosis and care that Eric was getting. It felt good to have Dr. Knarr there. We trusted him as a physician, and he understood our pain like few could, for he too had lost a child, his daughter, recently.

Everyone else left the room while he examined Eric and talked with us. We joined hands and with a cautious, deliberate, broken voice he began to express his own heartbreak and his grief for us. Judy and I latched onto him emotionally like a log in a torrential stream. Our souls bonded with his in those moments as he communicated so much in a few precious words. We knew that he understood and cared. His pain melded with ours and our hearts were joined in mutual love and respect.

Later we found out that was the first time Dr. Knarr had ever shared his feelings with anyone about his loss. Kyle's death and our grief were what it took to help our friend begin the process of mending his own broken heart.

Around midnight our good friend Andy came to see us. Like Brad, Andy lived next door to us. After some quiet conversation, Andy and I went out into the darkened hospital hallway and sat on the floor with our backs against the wall. There we talked softly well into the morning hours. At times there was silence for long stretches. At times we just cried. Then we would talk again and remember our many adventures with Kyle around the camp. The memories helped turn away some of the agonizing emptiness for a few moments. Then the tears would flow again.

As the night and early morning wore on, Judy and I agonized deep within our souls, grateful that X-rays had shown the baby unharmed, and hopeful for Eric—but dying with Kyle over and over in our minds and hearts. That day and night were not a nightmare. Would that they had been. The events that day were worse than any nightmare—they were real. Life would never be the same for our family. The beginning chapter of our happy family had come to an abrupt end.

Many things have changed since that gray, rainy

morning in 1979. Some of them are special joys for which we are so very thankful. But one thing is inescapable:

Kyle is gone—and so is a part of each of us.

Our lives have been changed . . . *forever*.

CHAPTER 3

The Agony of Empty Arms

One wept whose only child was dead,
New-born, ten years ago.
"Weep not; he is in bliss," they said.
She answered, "Even so,

Ten years ago was born in pain
A Child, not now forlorn
But oh, ten years ago, in vain
A Mother, a mother was born."

◆ An Unknown Mother

WHEN PEOPLE ARE FACED WITH *the death*, or the possibility of the death, of someone they love, they encounter a sea of turbulent emotions. You may be experiencing those emotions right now as our family did.

Unbelievable Dismay

In those lonely hours, waves of bewilderment, fear, frustration, and anger kept crashing against the shoreline of our family . . . pounding endlessly . . . powerfully . . . exhaustingly.

Kyle is dead and Eric is dying! Judy's announcement kept ringing in my head, bewildering my heart.

This couldn't be happening. Not to our family. Not to Kyle. Not to Eric. *I'll bargain with you, God! I cried. My life for theirs. Bring Kyle back. Keep Eric alive. Please!* Those were my muted words. The only response was a haunting quiet. There would be no arguing, bartering, or fighting to retrieve Kyle's life. I could do nothing for Eric. How could this be happening? Other people die . . . not me! . . . not mine! . . . not now!

In my experience, death was something we saw on television or read about in newspapers. Of course, as a pastor I knew of people who had died. And some more distant members of my own family had gone on, but death had never been this close.

Until it strikes someone with whom we have a close, vital relationship, we tend to think of death as something that happens to other people. To other families. Perhaps this is because our culture shields us from much of the death experience. Older people often die in hospitals and nursing homes rather than in their own houses with their families. Young men die in conflicts overseas. Even animals are taken away and put to sleep. So when we come face to face with death, it is an unbelievable visit.

We are stunned. It cannot be true. Yet our insides ache indescribably because we know that it is true. As James Sinacore notes, "The price we pay, inevitably, for leaving death entirely to other people is that when it eventually comes to us, it will take us by surprise, and find us shocked and unprepared. We will then, unavoidably, face it with bewilderment, anguish, and whatever denial we can muster."[1]

For anyone who has experienced the death of a loved one, either suddenly or after months or years of agonized waiting, there is a tenacious desire to deny reality, a desire that gives way only grudgingly as the minutes and days go by.

✦ ✦ ✦

As I sat in the emergency room of the hospital where they were trying to keep Eric alive, Bryan, our middle son, looked up at me. The words came very hard and slowly when Bryan cautiously asked, "Dad, is Eric going to die too?"

No! screamed my heart. My emotions yelled out against what I knew was a very real possibility—two can die as easily as one. All of me hoped that he would not die, but life carries no guarantees. We want them, but all the wishing and planning and money in the world cannot alter death's chosen visit. My response to Bryan was honest, but not complete.

"I don't know, Bryan," I said as I held him close. "I hope not." But even at his young age Bryan knew I was dodging the real question. He asked again, more pointedly still, "But can he?"

Yes! I cried inside, *I know he can. But surely he won't. Surely one is enough to satisfy death's appetite today.* But the words of Proverbs 27:20 rang in my heart, "Sheol and Abaddon are never satisfied" (NASB).

I was seeing death in a new way—not as an impersonal event, but as a personal enemy. For the first time I began to identify with the biblical writers who personify death and speak to it and about it as if it had a power and evil will of its own. The Psalmist exclaimed, "The cords of death entangled me. . . . I was overcome by trouble and sorrow" (Psalm 116:3).

My reply to Bryan again was honest but unrealistic, "Yes," I said, "he might die, Bryan. But I really don't believe he will. I really believe he will be okay."

What I was saying to Bryan was that I really did not want to believe that Eric could die. Face to face with Kyle's death, it was unbelievable to me that Eric would die also. I was feeling what one writer describes this way: "Despite the invincibility of death, we shall harbor a belief that it [can] be resisted and cajoled."[2]

✦ ✦ ✦

"Mr. Taylor, you have a phone call on line two."

"Thank you," I said as I picked up the phone.

"Hi, Rick. This is Cliff."

"Hello, Cliff."

". . . I just wanted to let you know that we have found Kyle's body in the pond. There was nothing we could do to save him. I'm so sorry, Rick," came Cliff's soft and tentative words.

"Who was that, Daddy?" asked Bryan.

"It was Cliff from the camp. They found Kyle. He is dead, Bryan." With those words, Bryan and I held on tight to each other, our eyes fixed on the ominous emergency room doors.

The Overwhelming Finality

Early the next morning word came that Eric was going to survive. However, we were warned that we would have to watch him neurologically for at least six years. Only time would tell if, and to what extent, his brain might have been affected. We were ecstatic that Eric was seemingly unharmed now, even if other things could show up later. But Eric's escape from danger brought the loss of our other son into even sharper focus. While Eric's life hung in the balance, our minds and emotions had to deal with conflicting thoughts and feelings about both boys. We were too deeply in shock to fully realize what had happened. But as Eric's condition improved, the truth began to penetrate: Kyle was gone.

The first reality that we had to face, and that everyone faces when the shock of death begins to subside, is that the person we loved so much was not coming back. Death is not a temporary vacation. There is no negotiating with death. From a human perspective, death is the enemy and its victory certain.[3]

Those who are left behind wrestle with conflicting emotions—wanting to bring their loved one back, but knowing that they cannot. I used to dream repeatedly that I was jumping into that muddy pond, saving my son's life. I was determined in my dream to find him and save him—save him from the finalness of death. I wanted the last word on death, but I could not have it. I was crushed inside, defeated. My dreams turned to nightmares again and again. Death seemed to mock me and taunt me. It would let me dream, but only so it could throw the reality of death's finality back into my face again.

If there had been any greater joy for Judy and me than discovering we had arms for holding, mending, soothing, loving, and helping, it was the delight that had come from actually using them. And for more than five years our parental arms had been full. We had loved it. We had celebrated the life of full arms! But as the reality of Kyle's death began to penetrate my shock, I was instantly drained of something . . . a part of me . . . of who I am. I felt empty. The arms of my heart ached to hold him one more time—just once! But it was not to be.

In the months ahead I would encounter the kind of inner turmoil I had never imagined possible, and I would struggle to regain some equilibrium in my life as a husband, as a father, and as a person.

CHAPTER 4

The Raging of a Tormented Soul

What I feared has come upon me;
*   what I dreaded has happened to me.*
I have no peace, no quietness;
*   I have no rest, but only turmoil.*

✦ Job 3:25,26

WHEN JUDY AND I brought Eric home from the hospital, we met the unexpected. All of the treasured possessions Kyle had used to express his aliveness were waiting for us: his clothes lying on the floor, his watercolor painting on the refrigerator door, his baseball bat leaning against the tree in the backyard. On top of the television sat a red, white, and black Lego house that Kyle had made a few days earlier. He had told us that he was not going to live in the new home I was building, but would live in one like his Lego house—next door, but close to us. All the remnants of Kyle's aliveness were right there, just waiting for his return.

In the days that followed, I felt my son's absence keenly. Life was somehow different. I was different. Something was happening inside me that I could not explain.

Whatever it was, it was growing. Judy noticed it. Other friends began to notice it as well. I found myself expressing stronger feelings about many things than ever before. I could not hold my emotions back. It was as if all the passions of my life had been unleashed. It was not simply that I was freer to express my emotions—I couldn't keep them inside any longer.

One of those emotions, though I tried to deny it, was anger. Rage was brewing inside me. I had never experienced such pitched, intense feelings before. Perhaps you are experiencing the same types of feelings. You may have tried to figure out who you are angry with and come up short. Are you angry with God? You may be. I was, and I would grapple with that anger for many months. Are you angry with the doctor, or the person who was driving the other car, or yourself? Any of these may be true, but for me, and perhaps for you as well, there was yet another anger, a deeper one that I hadn't recognized before.

Over time I began to realize that anger is an emotion God designed to go into action when we perceive injustice. And believe me, I had perceived injustice to the very root of my being.

Though it would be some time between when I first felt these emotions and when I finally understood them, I know now that it was death itself that I perceived as wrong. My emotions had brought my erroneous beliefs to the surface, letting me know that something was desperately amiss. I had always pictured death as natural, since all people die; good, since God decreed it; and dignified—something that comes quietly at a point later in life. I was wrong on all counts.

Death Is Not Natural

Admittedly death is real. But we should not confuse the fact that death is predictable and universal to mean that it is natural. There are many things in this world that are predictable and universal. Greed and lust and pride and abuse and prejudice are all predictable and universal, and yet we call these abnormal and unnatural. These are seen as flaws in humankind.

It was not natural for my 5½-year-old son's life to be snatched away and ended. It is not natural for a husband to lose his wife while their children are still young and dependent on her, or for a father to fall to a heart attack in the prime of his life, or for a lifelong companion to die just as the golden years are beginning.

Most people instinctively recognize that the death of a young person is unnatural. But consider for a moment the possibility that all death is unnatural. The design of our bodies is to live and grow and develop. Most of us never develop more than 5 percent of our mental capacities, and 100 years of life is premature in light of our bodies' "natural" design capabilities. Death, when it comes, usually results from disease or accident or malfunction.

If I can dream endless dreams, draw endless plans, think endless thoughts, then why cannot I, and those I love, live on endlessly? All of our experience in living shouts to us that death is cutting short our design. We do not exist just to be buried and decompose. Though we live in a time when we are constantly being told that we are merely sophisticated animals and that death is natural, there is still something inside us that rallies up when we stand face to face with death.

God designed Adam and Eve—humankind—expressly to have a living relationship with Him. God did not design us to be disposable. Death came because of man's choice, not God's original design: "Sin entered the world through one man, and death through sin, and in this way death came to all men, because all sinned" (Romans 5:12).

Death was not intended by God to be a natural part of life. It was intended to be an ominous reminder of sin and a warning of judgment. As researchers Larry Richards and Paul Johnson have said concerning death: "God's warning to Adam and Eve in the garden was a presentation of life, contrasted with a choice that would lead to death. Throughout Scripture where life and death are contrasted, death is always the one from which we're to turn away."[1]

One reason I was angry was because death is not the purpose for which we were designed. Death is an end to what is natural, not a part of it. Life is natural. Death is not!

Death Is Not Good

Another reason I was growing increasingly angry was that everything in me cries out that death is not good. "Good" is not rude and ruthless. "Good" does not surprise and steal life. "Good" gives—death takes. When a woman has lost her husband to cancer, it is thoughtless to try to show her how much good will come from it.

"Think of the freedom you will have now."

"Just rest in the fact that he is in a better place."

"You will be a deeper and more compassionate person for having gone through this yourself."

Even though these things may be true, the woman facing the death of her husband is shattered and crushed. Her world has just caved in. Her life has been changed forever! Good may come out of bad situations, but bad is bad, not good. We should not confuse that.

No one will ever convince me that drowning in a murky lake is good. Death made Kyle suffer needlessly. Death made our remaining sons agonize for many months. Death left Judy and me empty and sick inside. Death ended something very good.

Focusing on the "good" in death can be a subtle form of denial. We are not being honest with ourselves or others if we refuse to recognize the inherent badness of death. "Death is associated with sin. So is guilt. The flood of feelings that may come are simply evidence of the linkage of these great enemies of man."[2]

Unless we face this honestly we will never be able to face death fully or help others in an empathetic way.

Empathy is "feeling with" someone. And a person facing death, either their own or that of someone close, inherently feels that death is wrong, not right. If we do not allow ourselves to feel that death is malicious, then we will not be able to feel with others and help them in their grief. Only as we truly understand this will we be able to weep with those who weep.

Over the years many people have entered our lives who have walked this same path—some of them in Death and Dying classes where we have spoken, some as a result of our being guests on television programs, and others when we have spoken at various types of "helping" meetings. We do not have to know these people intimately to feel their pain. People who have lost someone dear become members of a club not volunteered for, and in which the camaraderie and compassion run deep.

The growing rage inside me toward death was my heart's way of identifying with the heart of God: "I take no pleasure in the death of anyone, declares the Sovereign Lord. Repent and live" (Ezekiel 18:32). God takes pleasure in what is good. He does not take pleasure in the death of His people, and neither should we.

Death Is Not Dignified

But there was yet another reason for my anger toward death. Death enters our lives without knocking. As one researcher into death has said, "Death is a social disease, like V.D. It is not polite, not well-mannered."[3] It never asks permission and it never asks our opinion on timing. King Solomon concurred: "No man has authority to restrain the wind . . . or authority over the day of death" (Ecclesiastes 8:8).

For many of us, life is like a big game. The object of the game is to do everything we can not to land on the square marked "death." We reach for immortality by eating right, exercising, driving defensively, and the list goes on. And yet, no matter how healthy or safety-conscious we are, the thief called death ultimately steals our life away. Again Solomon writes:

> I again saw under the sun that the race is not to the swift, and the battle is not to the warriors, and neither is bread to the wise, nor wealth to the discerning, nor favor to men of ability; for time and chance overtake them all.
>
> Moreover, man does not know his time: like fish caught in a treacherous net, and birds trapped in a snare, so the sons of men are ensnared at an evil time when it suddenly falls on them" (Ecclesiastes 9:11,12 NASB).

Death robs from all people their most valuable possession—life. Even a person who hates life and chooses to end it himself has the opportunity to choose such an alternative because he is alive. But what choices do we have in death? Death eliminates *all* freedom of choice. Death chooses and death dictates. There is no democracy in death. No wonder we are willing to try almost anything to avoid it. Even the Psalmist shared this desire:

> My heart is in anguish within me, and the terrors of death have fallen upon me. Fear and trembling come upon me: and horror has overwhelmed me. And I said, "Oh, that I had wings like a dove! I would fly away and be at rest. Behold, I would wander far away; I would lodge in the wilderness. I would hasten to my place of refuge from the stormy wind and tempest" (Psalm 55:4-8 NASB).

Not only is death ruthless in dealing with us personally, but also with those around us. A son or daughter, a father or mother, an aunt or uncle or a close friend—all these can be snatched by death without warning. Death never lets us forget it is there, waiting for us and those we love the most.

God did not design death to be natural and normal ...just another experience in the phases of life. He wanted it to seize our attention, shake our souls, and enrage our passions.

I hate death because it is not natural, not good, and certainly not dignified. It is not God's design, but the result of man's choice. What a horrid choice we have made! I am seized, shaken and enraged at the horror of death...and rightly I should be. Death is constantly changing our world. And because of the death of someone near, our lives will never be the same.

CHAPTER 5

Why Can't
I Rejoice?

Joy is gone from our hearts;
our dancing has turned to mourning.

◆ Lamentations 5:15

WHEN KYLE DIED I found comfort and assurance in the
fact that he was with his heavenly Father, a Father far
better than I had ever been or ever could be. I was
relieved for him. But I was not with him. Though he was
with a better Father, I was still his father, too. The relationship between us did not change; just the opportunity to enjoy that relationship. Part of me was gone
and irretrievably lost for the rest of my life.

As we have seen, many people who have the assurance that their loved one is with the heavenly Father
come to the conclusion that death is a normal part of life
and therefore must be good. Scripture is often used to
support this reasoning. For example, we turn to Philippians 1:21 and read, "For to me, to live is Christ and to
die is gain." Our minds also jump to Romans 8:28 where
Paul teaches us that "God causes all things to work
together for good" (NASB).

Based on these and other Scriptures of hope for our
life after death, we turn funerals into celebrations. We
celebrate the gain for our loved one who has gone on
before us. We indeed do not need to, nor should we,
grieve as those who have no hope. But just as a funeral is
a celebration for the gain of the Christian who has gone
to be with his heavenly Father, so also a funeral or

41

memorial service cements the finality of loss to the ones left behind.

On the Wednesday after Kyle's death, we had a memorial service at the camp dining hall. Many local people came, as well as friends from other parts of the country, to be with us on this especially difficult day. Judy and I were overwhelmed by the friendship and support of so many wonderful people. We were honored by the sense of reunion. We were dismayed at the occasion that brought all these friends to one place at this time.

At the service we played some of Kyle's favorite songs. Judy and I spent time sharing our reflections on Kyle's 5½ years of life. We felt compelled to proclaim the value of our son's life, but we were dying inside, wondering how we would be able to go on from there. We asked people to pray for our family at the service, and it meant so much to feel the support and love of so many through their prayers. There was a tremendous bond of love in the air as the service ended.

As the day wore on, however, most of the people left to go home. Each took with them part of Kyle's memories. With friends leaving, memories fleeting, and Kyle gone forever, we began to feel empty and alone. Somehow the part of me that ached to be a dad to Kyle did not feel that death should be a celebration. I could not rejoice. I could only weep. Yet because of the expectations I held as a Christian, I felt pressure to rejoice at something that did not make me joyful. In the coming weeks, several of our closest Christian friends and family were able to weep with us. Many, however, were as unprepared to deal with our grief as we were.

It was during this time that I personally realized that the "gain" in Philippians 1:21 was for the one dying. That verse was not speaking to *me* but to *Kyle*. And what a relief it was to get beneath the surface of Romans 8:28. God wasn't saying that all things *are* good, but that he *will bring* good out of all things. What a difference! I no longer had to feel guilty about my pain.

It often seems that one of the measures of a mature Christian regarding death is how much we rejoice and how little we cry. Pain and hurt and difficulty are not supposed to dent our spiritual armor . . . at least not too bad . . . not too long. There is some tolerance for grief, but not much.

The longer we grieve, the "weaker" we appear. But biblical Christianity makes a distinction between "grieving" and "grieving without hope" (1 Thessalonians 4:13). Grief over loss is something natural and normal. It is something we ought to do. Even Jesus, standing before the tomb of Lazarus, knowing Lazarus would be alive again within minutes, still wept (John 11:1-53). The grief of loss agonized Jesus. Paul tells us all that we ought to weep with those who weep (Romans 12:15). And we ought to comfort other Christians in their times of distress (2 Corinthians 1:3-7). So why is it so hard for many of us as Christians to accept and respond appropriately to normal, natural grief in ourselves or in another person?

Maybe part of the reason is that we have picked up lessons from the world. Listen to this evaluation of our secular society:

> In our society people are full of admiration for the bereaved who keep "a stiff upper lip" and behave "maturely." Even if this is not put into words, the implicit demand on people is not to let themselves go. This may well collude with the mourner's own defenses and increase his denial of a need to grieve.[1]

It is interesting to apply Paul's admonition, "Do not conform any longer to the pattern of this world, but be transformed by the renewing of your mind" (Romans

12:2), to the subject of death and grief. Everyone has been or will be affected by death many times in a lifetime. But when was the last time you attended a series of biblical talks on death, whether a preaching series, a class, or a small group study? When was the last time you even heard of such a thing? How many of us are knocking on the pastor's door asking for that kind of teaching to renew our minds? Honestly, death and death's grief make us uncomfortable. We avoid it, and somehow hope it will avoid us.

Like me, you may feel caught between a rock and a hard place in your own heartache. You may feel that if you don't celebrate, you will be in double jeopardy—not only aching over your loss, but also fearing condemnation from more "spiritual" friends and family for your inability to rejoice.

May I encourage you? If you cannot celebrate right now, there is nothing wrong with you. The day will come when you begin to see God's loving hand bringing good from a terrible event, but for now, don't be ashamed to grieve. In doing so you will give those who are uncomfortable with your grief a chance to move toward maturity in this area of life as well.

Embrace the sorrow. Don't fight back the tears. Let them flow when they are there. Don't avoid thinking about your lost one. Pull out the photo album. Take time to remember. Be willing to talk about your sense of loss and pain with someone else. In doing these things, you will prevent a festering wound that would eventually spread infection to every area of your life.

CHAPTER 6

The Battle to Get Back to Normal

*Being crushed means
being reshaped . . .*

♦ Charles R. Swindoll

IN THE MONTHS THAT FOLLOWED Kyle's death I felt like a man who had been deeply wounded, trying to recover. As I looked in the mirror of my life I desperately wanted to look like "me"—the old "me"—the "me" before April 7. Normally an easygoing person, my newly unleashed emotions were like raw nerve endings, set off at the slightest little things: seeing a pond or lake, watching one of our boys dive into a swimming pool, seeing the tub fill with water. My emotions would immediately begin to swell, my eyes would flood, and the agony of my empty arms would be fresh and new. I was uneasy with these new emotions. I wanted them to settle back down into the recesses of my life.

Two months after Kyle's death, Judy gave birth to our little girl, Kelly Christine. It was about that time when I began to build our home. I welcomed the busyness. I found it refreshing to pound the nails . . . harder . . . and harder. It kept me so busy I did not have to look into the mirror—the mirror that kept showing me I was changing.

On those occasions when I would catch my "changing" reflection, I wrote it off as a baby, a new house, so much busyness. *When things settle down, so will I. I'll get back to normal.* I had been wounded, but now I was ready to recover. What I didn't realize, or at least did not want to admit, was that my wound was permanent. Part of me, and mine, was gone . . . never to return in my lifetime. I would *never* be the person I was before.

The more I denied this changed life, the worse things got. Accepting and going along with the changes would not make the pain of loss go away, but until I began to understand the nature of these changes in my life and in the lives of others, I could not make the most of the life I had yet to live.

Responding to the Changed Life

As was mentioned earlier, when our son died my wife and I dealt with our loss in very different ways. Judy had devoted the past six years of her life to teaching Kyle how to crawl and walk and talk and count and color. Much of her thinking, day in and day out, revolved around helping Kyle grow and learn and develop. Suddenly and shockingly her firstborn was gone. Part of Judy died that day. She kept hanging on to precious memories and her last recollections of her son, the things he had done and the things they had done together. She cherished and pondered each little bit of Kyle she would find in the unfinished coloring book or in a note found tucked beneath the cushions of the couch.

I was very different. I too remembered and cherished my last days with my son. But most of all I was struggling with the anger inside. Along with my anger toward death itself, I was also angry because Kyle's death seemed so unnecessary and unjust. "Why did this have to happen to Kyle?" "Why not me instead?" "How could God allow such an atrocity?" I was angry at the seemingly cruel injustice that had stolen our oldest son. I wanted some answers and I knew I would not rest until I found them.

Because of our different personalities, we experienced and dealt with the emotions of death in unique ways. Judy needed to keep talking about her recollections of Kyle. I needed to think, and study, and wrestle. For me to keep on talking about our son's death was deeply frustrating. Not surprisingly, this affected our family unity and put an enormous strain on our marriage relationship. There were no major fights; just busyness, coping, and silence. Judy took care of the baby, and I built the new house. Judy went to town for supplies alone, and I kept hammering. Judy was grateful for Kelly's colic in the middle of sleepless nights, and I was glad when I was alone and not being asked to talk about it all. We were still kind to each other. There were no raised voices. But we were stressed, frustrated, hurting people.

Judy felt she needed me to share my hurting feelings, but when she approached me she felt guilty for bringing up things that seemed to reopen a gaping wound in me. She felt like she was stabbing her best friend. At the same time I felt guilt and shame for avoiding her questions and not being able to meet her needs. I could see my silence was hurting the person I loved more than anything, and yet I could not seem to muster what it took to talk about it with her.

Like us, each person who faces a death thinks, feels, and responds uniquely to his or her changed and changing life. Some grow cold and callous, refusing to admit their devastated emotions. Some do nothing but weep and wonder. Some people want to talk while others want to be alone and quiet. Some people establish memorials to a lost one while others put away everything that reminds them of that person.

Some people will be very active and some extremely inactive. There may be sharp swings. One day you may be greatly comforted by having friends come and show concern, but a day later feel that you will go mad if you cannot be alone for a few minutes or hours.

All of this is normal. We each face death in our own way, and it's right that we should. There is no "right" way to deal with death. Everyone has their own ideas about how to deal with the death of a loved one. Unfortunately, we often assume that our way is the best way for everyone, when in truth each individual is unique and their relationship with the one who has died is also unique. Sometimes our unique relationships necessitate very different ways of dealing with the loss. And at times these individual ways collide.

We each do the best we can, yet none of us feels like it's just right or quite enough. For example, Judy and I had only a couple of hours while waiting at the hospital with Eric to make decisions about Kyle's funeral and a host of other things we had never thought about before. Fortunately, we quickly agreed with each other. We did not want to have a funeral and graveside service; we wanted to remember Kyle alive. Kyle's body was buried the next day, and instead of a funeral we had a memorial service several days later that was very meaningful to our family.

Kyle's schoolteacher, however, was extremely upset that we had not had a viewing of the body so that she could say goodbye. We understood, but that was not what we had needed right then. Other people wondered what kind of parents we were for not wanting to be there when Kyle's body was placed in the ground in that small casket.

We would never say that what we chose to do is right for everybody. Never! But it was right for us. We were sorry that it was not what fit with other people's needs and feelings and beliefs, but we did the best we could.

We need to realize the individual difficulties facing each person, and allow others to cope with death in their own way. Little is accomplished in trying to help someone deal with death "better." Devastation and loss have to be worked out by each person. No one can do it for them—nor should they try. But we can help by being accepting and understanding.

After about six months, Judy and I began to understand and respect each other's needs and ways of dealing with Kyle's death. By then I had worked through many of the questions that had plagued me. I was more willing to begin talking, and she was more willing to talk not only about what I felt, but also what I was wrestling with in my mind. In turn, I began to ask her how she was feeling and gave her the freedom to express her hurt and agony.

Understanding Changed Relationships

I did not volunteer the death of my son. I did not invite this stranger of change into my home. But it had come, uninvited, and with it a new relationship with everyone else who was a part of our lives. In the battle to get back to normal, many of these relationships became stronger. Some of them grew weaker. All of them changed.

We noticed our changed relationships in a hundred ways. Easter fell just eight days after Kyle's death. Our family wanted and needed to be in church on that day. But it was immediately obvious that we made many people uncomfortable. They didn't know what to say, or what not to say.

Then the pastor stood up to speak about the glorious event in history that dealt with sin and death in an ultimate way. It was a small congregation and we were sitting on the front row, yet not one word was spoken to us or for us. Not a word was uttered about our death or our hope in Christ's resurrection. The discomfort we experienced wasn't the result of maliciousness; people simply didn't know what to do.

We left hurriedly to get back to the camp, hoping to rid ourselves of the strain we felt at church. We arrived a little late for lunch. The dining hall was already buzzing with conversation and the sounds of dishes being passed and food being served.

As we walked through the room, a hush fell over the cheerful crowd. Eyes turned, heads nodded in our direction. They cared. But we felt "un-normal" and isolated. We had not only lost a son, but also "the way life was."

When C.S. Lewis lost his wife, he kept a diary of his feelings. In one of his entries, he captured the awkwardness and isolation that came his way with the death of someone near:

> An odd byproduct of my loss is that I'm aware of being an embarrassment to everyone I meet. At work, at the club, in the street, I see people, as they approach me, trying to make up their minds whether they'll "say something about it" or not. I hate it if they do, and if they don't. Some funk it altogether. R. has been avoiding me for a week. I like best the well-brought-up young men, almost boys, who walk up to me as if I were a dentist, turn very red, get it over, and then edge away to the bar as quickly as they decently can. Perhaps the bereaved ought to be isolated in special settlements like lepers.[1]

In my search for normalcy at church and at camp, I found disappointment and frustration from the hands of well-meaning people who had also been forced to deal with an unwanted change.

All who experience the loss of a loved one find themselves in similar situations. Until we accept the reality that God wants to change our lives—that we can never return to a former way of life because an essential part of that life is gone—our natural tendency will be to resist and fight what we perceive to be a foreign invader. The sooner we realize that our lives have been changed for-ever, the sooner we find the freedom to experience our changed and changing relationships.

Embracing What Time Can't Change

As Judy and I struggled with feelings of isolation, we discovered that time doesn't really heal the wounds. Time does not take away the agony and suffering, the sense of loss and aloneness. To rely on time changing those strong feelings is like moving into the wrong house. Eventually you have to move again, and the change is even more difficult. The poet E. Millay heard the rumor that time heals, and unfortunately believed it. When he finally realized the rumor was a lie, he cried out:

> Time does not bring relief; you have all lied
> Who told me time would ease me of my pain!
> ... But last year's bitter loving must remain
> Heaped on my heart, and my thoughts abide.[2]

When we face the death of someone near, our lives are changed—and continually changing—from then on. Death rips from us a significant part of what went into making our lives what we called "normal." Some of life's most prized possessions have been cruelly snatched away—things like laughter and winks and little kisses on the cheek, and voices that will never again say, "I love you." Death robs us of these living possessions. How can life ever be the same again? It can't!

But even more than that, the death of someone near sets off a perpetual chain of dominoes in our lives. When Kyle died, one area of our lives after another was touched and changed. Some of our friendships were built around Kyle's friendships and activities. Suddenly those rela-tionships were being affected. Judy no longer had her chief helper with the other two boys. And the boys no longer had someone to tell them when to go to sleep and brush their teeth. They kept finding themselves one man short in the games they always played.

Death is the single most devastating event that will ever affect a person. And once that event takes place we are continually forced to deal with it over and over. Faced with the perpetual nature of change, some people choose to ignore it. But in their efforts to avoid it, they change. They may become more lonely and isolated or angry and bitter, always trying to recapture what is gone forever: normal.

Others create memorials to try to replace the lost loved one. In doing so, they change. They may turn the person's room into a shrine, trying desperately to keep something of that person alive. But pictures do not talk, and clothes on hangers cannot give hugs as before. The person may become continually sad and depressed, always looking for what is gone: normal.

Some people try to replace their loss with another child, another mate, another friend. But no one can truly replace a lost loved one. In trying to make the impossible happen, they change. Loss hurts. It is the hurt in life that we hope to soothe, hope to quiet and cover, hope to repair and recover from as quickly as possible. It is difficult to welcome and accept losses; rather, we seek more to hold on to what we had in the past.

Our friends and family, and we ourselves, wanted us to get back to "normal." But "normal" had been fiendishly changed. And the longer we were different than we had been, the longer we grieved, the more uncomfortable all of us became and the more we struggled with times of helpless guilt.

We had a very static view of life. In time we began to learn that true biblical Christian living is dynamic, not static. It is always changing. God sees to that! "Consider it all joy, my brothers," the apostle James says, "whenever you face trials of many kinds" (James 1:2). Life is a path that constantly presents the traveler with new situations and varied circumstances, and the journey requires constant adjustment. God wants us as Christians to be growing and stretching. It is not the stable, settled, static times in our lives that produce the growth and change that we need; it is the difficult times.

After Kyle died there came a time when Judy and I realized our lives had been changed forever. At first we regretted that we could not go back to the way we were before Kyle died. We felt as though we had not only lost our son, and a part of us with him, but also the life we knew. We had lost the "normalcy" that we had grown to enjoy. That grieved us, too.

Normal had been redefined, without our wishing or wanting it. And we knew down deep inside that the old normal would never be possible again. But it also became very obvious to us that what we had thought of as normal was a phantom. It existed only in our minds. The reality was that each day promises a fresh beginning, and the only real constant is God and His new love each morning. That was what we needed and learned to count on.

Time doesn't heal, but God comforts and refreshes us over time when we let Him. We still live with our sense of loss for Kyle. That will never go away. But our faith has grown as we have learned to resist the temptation to return to our old sense of "normalcy." God has used our grief—our pain and our agony—to make us deeper, richer people. We are not the people we used to be, and for that we are thankful. Instead we are closer to being the people that God wants us to be, and the people that we long to be.

I began to cooperate with this process of change with a mixture of feelings. I felt relieved and excited about the growth in my life. I also experienced guilt. Did it take the death of my son to make me change and grow? Did my son experience death so I could mature as a person? What a horrid possibility!

God used Kyle's death to change my life, but Kyle did not die because of me. You see, even our thoughts that happy, healthy children shouldn't die is a giveaway of our belief that life should be static, stable, and predictable. It is not. Life changes.

There is no getting over, getting around, or getting by the loss of a loved one. Our lives by definition are changed, and by experience are changing. And the more we understand the true nature of death, the better prepared we will be to make the most of our constantly changing lives.

Facing Death

The paradox is that when you accept the fact of death, you are freed to live.
But accepting the fact of death, finding its meaning, facing it squarely: This is not the same as becoming obsessed with it.

—Joseph Bayly

CHAPTER 7

A Frustrating Faith

*I had firmly planted the ladder of my faith on
the wrong wall.*

I WAS NOT PREPARED to deal with the death of my son.
Though I was a pastor and had counseled many people
in the grief and loss that accompanies death, and though
I had been a Christian for many years—I simply wasn't
prepared. My Christian faith seemed to have let me
down. Or had it? During the time after Kyle's death
when I was looking for answers to my many questions, I
began to wonder: Just what is a Christian *supposed* to
believe about death? Were some ways I'd been taught to
look at death incomplete or simply wrong? Did I really
have a biblical view of death and dying?

In my journey through grief, I had a driving need to
find resolutions that satisfied my mind as well as my
emotions. And so I began a search to understand more
clearly what Scripture teaches about death. Slowly I
learned to recognize misconceptions in what I had been
taught. I began to understand how the world's view of
death had subtly influenced my own perceptions. And I
realized how blurred our image of God can sometimes
become. In going through this process, I learned to avoid
some of the detours that can seem so enticing as a person
travels through the valley of the shadow of death. What
I've discovered is that Scripture provides a sure and

stable roadmap for anyone whose life has been changed forever by the death of someone near.

In this chapter we will look at some of the misconceptions people have about death. In the chapters that follow we will look at the world's view of death, some distortions that can cloud our perception of God and influence our view of death, and finally, what the biblical view of death really is.

Misconception 1: Death Is Only a Deadline

So much of what we as Christians are taught about death is true and accurate, but cold and calculated—more like a legal brief than an empathetic note. And nearly all of what we learn has to do with what comes after death.

When many Christians think about death, they think of it as simply the deadline God has given for us to make a decision about eternity. That is true theologically, biblically. But it does not deal with what death is and the grief of those left behind. It is only part of the whole truth.

Before Kyle drowned in that murky lake, I thought very little about death. Heaven was secure. I had reserved a room for eternity in advance. Quite rightly, I and my family had planned adequately for "after" death, never realizing there was a "during" death—the time between when a loved one dies and when we might be with him or her again in heaven.

For the person desperately trying to adjust to the loss of a loved one, all the future personal security in the world takes a back seat to the present pain. The aching heart drowns out all other thoughts and hopes. The death of a loved one makes us deal with the unbelievable pain in the here-and-now. Suddenly, in the midst of emptiness the familiar child's prayer seems lacking: "Now I lay me down to sleep; I pray the Lord my soul to keep; If I should die before I wake; I pray the Lord my soul to take."

Kyle died. God took his soul. But what about his parents, brothers, family, and friends? Our souls were kept, but not taken. It was a painful way to learn that there was more to death than dying.

Misconception 2: Bad Things Don't Happen to Good Christians

Most people would never admit it. They would never say it aloud. But many Christians live under the delusion that bad things don't, or at least shouldn't, happen to "good" Christians—those people who appear to be doing all of the right things to earn God's favor. Of course the Bible teaches that "all have sinned and fall short of the glory of God" (Romans 3:23). God's gifts to us are not based on our personal merit. Yet when an apparent "bad thing" happens, like the death of someone who has made life better, richer, and deeper, our responses betray us. One way we respond is to convince ourselves that death is not really bad after all. In some way death must be good. We just don't feel that way. Because we do not want to believe that bad things happen to "good" Christians, we allow our wills to convince our minds that what is obviously bad and ruthless and ravaging is actually good. And as we saw earlier, in a sense it is good—for the person who is now at home with the Lord (Philippians 1:21). But for those left behind it is a devastating experience. God can use the experience for good in our lives, but that does not make the event itself good.

Another way that our misconceptions are exposed is when we respond to death by saying or implying that the person must not have been a "good" Christian after all. If the badness of death cannot be dismissed, this becomes a convenient way to deal with the emotions caused by our misguided faith. There must have been something wrong with the person that brought on this horrid fate.

I'll never forget the time shortly after Kyle's death when a dear friend tried to console us by saying, "You never know how Kyle might have turned out. He was a neat kid now, but you just don't know; he may have been a real rebellious rascal in his later years. Maybe he would have brought a great deal of heartache and misery upon himself and you. God is probably sparing you and Judy from some rebellious teenage years ahead." This woman didn't mean to sound cruel. She just could not accept the reality that bad things happen to "good" Christians or that pain is part of life for everyone who lives in a fallen world.

Misconception 3: God Is Unfair

Yet another sign that we have further to go in our understanding of death is our anger toward God. When we secretly believe that bad things don't happen to "good" Christians, we may feel that God has played a dirty trick on us. He has changed the rules. He has been unfair (to the "good" Christians) and unjust (by allowing something bad to happen). If we can't change bad circumstances to good circumstances, or good Christians to bad Christians to justify our own perspective, then we get furious with God because he is disturbing what we have quietly grown to accept as truth: our own unwritten laws.

The longer I live, the more I realize how easy and natural it is for human beings to condense everything down to simple, easy-to-remember lists, laws, and formulas. The Pharisees of Jesus' day condensed all of the Old Testament into a list of rules to which they added their own explanations of meaning. So intent on their own agenda were they that when God came into their midst, many of them could not recognize or accept Him. They were out of touch with the reality of God and His life.

As Christians, we can unintentionally do the same kinds of things. We can easily boil the Christian faith down into a few key principles for living. The danger comes when we start to look to our lists of beliefs as our authority, rather than to God Himself, who speaks to us through His Word. When it seems that God is reneging on His end of the bargain (a bargain He never made) we feel justified in our anger, when instead we should be learning to live by faith in who He is and continually searching the Scriptures so that He can show us more clearly what He has said.

The disciples asked Jesus whose sin caused a man to be blind, his own or his parents. Jesus said it wasn't one or the other, but it had happened so that "the work of God might be displayed in his life" (John 9:3). Not man's work, in keeping the law, but God's work. God allows unexpected, unexplainable, undesirably bad things to happen, even to Christians who are growing in Christ, so that we might be brought closer to Him, not only as Savior but as the Lord of life—and death.

I had placed my faith in some faulty misconceptions of what Christianity said about death. I had listened to what people said rather than to God. I had unknowingly placed my ladder of faith on the wrong wall. And, for me, that wall of misconceptions collapsed the very instant I stood face to face with death. My frustration grew.

Since Kyle's death, my faith has changed. I have put my ladder of faith on a different wall, one that accepts change and dynamic differences as part of a relationship with a living Savior and His eternal Word. This wall rejects the idea that pain and suffering are the destroyers of life, but rather, in God's hands, the chisel and hammer that forge a stronger foundation for life.

Misconception 4: We Feel What We Know

It would be months before I would begin to understand that God was just and loving, and that He does cause all things to work together for my good. Even though I was convinced in my mind that Kyle was in a better place, under better care, and waiting for our arrival, I found myself under a great weight of guilt. I was living under the frustrating belief that we feel what we know.

Knowledge and feelings do go hand in hand. However, they are seldom on the same timetable! Our minds resemble computers that take in data, facts, figures, and evidence and then sort and weigh this input to come to a conclusion. But our feelings are vastly different. They resemble deep wells that collect the waters of perceived truth from our minds and store them deep within. The mind can take in new information and evidences and quickly adapt. But our emotions change very slowly and reluctantly.

If you have ever narrowly avoided a car accident or been frightened late at night by the rustling of tree branches, you realize that it takes only a second or two for our minds to adjust and yell to our emotions, "False alarm!" However, it takes several minutes for our hearts to stop pounding and our nerves to get off edge.

To use another illustration, when I became a Christian one of the first things I began to understand was that I was forgiven by God. However, after all these years, my emotions still wrestle with feeling the forgiveness that my mind knows is true. Feelings run deeper and change more slowly than knowledge.

The closer we are to someone and the deeper our bond of love, the longer it will take for our emotions to adjust and mend from the awful wound of death. That is why those who aren't as close to the person who died may wonder why it is taking you so long to recover. Their adjustment may have been accomplished weeks or months or even years earlier.

I will never forget one lady with whom I counseled who was still deeply grieving the sudden loss of her husband. After several months, Betty's family began to shun her and tell her that it was high time she get past her grief. It was easier for them because they had not been as close to Betty's husband as she had been. As Betty better understood God and His ability and willingness to go through grief with her, her *mind* began to change. But it was many months before Betty began to *feel* what she knew to be true.

Time does not heal, but it does take time for our wounded emotions to adjust and adapt—much longer than for our minds. Waiting for our feelings to catch up with our knowledge requires patience. Sometimes a lot of it. That was a long and painful lesson to learn. In the midst of learning this lesson, I found very little to rejoice about. But that was acceptable, at least for a time—at least to God and me.

CHAPTER 8

Facts and Fictions

Do not conform any longer to the pattern of this world, but be transformed by the renewing of your mind.

✦ Romans 12:2

AS EACH OF US GRAPPLES with the loss of a loved one, we face a chorus of voices telling us how we should go about "understanding death." Some of these voices are very subtle. Like the incomplete Christian teaching that left me unprepared to face the death of my son, they come from deep in our past and leave us frustrated and floundering.

But there are other voices—loud, inconsistent, worldly voices from which we instinctively turn away. Yet because of their volume and constant, resonant beat, we cannot help hearing and listening. Even without our conscious awareness, bits and pieces of these fictions from the world have a way of etching themselves into the fiber of our being.

Because each of these discordant voices is essentially untrue, it ends on the note of hopelessness. But each of them have just enough fact in them to catch our imagination. And if we allow our minds to take the bait, we discover quite a hook underneath.

More than one of these voices from the world affected me, and I realized it only as I struggled to survive Kyle's death. You may also find yourself tempted to believe one or more of these lies as you struggle with your loss, or friends and family members may be convinced that some of them are true. In exposing these fictions to the light of truth, you will be able to better understand them and guard your own heart, perhaps helping someone else in the process.

Death Can Be Ignored

Probably the most deceptive and common fiction of all is that we can build a protective wall around our hearts that refuses to let death in. In a *Time* magazine interview, Woody Allen gave this personal advice: "You have to deny the reality of death to go on every day."[1]

This fiction admits that death is truly awesome. It can even admit that death matters and that it may not be safe. But it concludes, because it has nothing better to offer, that ignoring death should be our goal. The better we can convince ourselves that death really is not there, the freer we are to enjoy life now.

How effective this fiction is depends on a person's ability to trick his mind and dismiss his feelings. But this can be difficult. Our minds have been designed by God to detect trickery: Memory, logic, and reason all join to defeat a person's desire to deceive his own mind. However, for those who can temporarily succeed, this self-defeating way of thinking can become one of the most inwardly devastating of all the worldly voices. And it seems to be equally attractive to Christians and people of other faiths. At its core it robs people of passionately enjoying life, for it is only in dealing with an enemy like death that we can ever be free to truly enjoy life and living.

It is true that we should not be preoccupied with death. We should wrap our lives around the Lord and His kingdom, and develop other interests in our work and hobbies and relationships. Death needs to be faced head-on, but not in a morbid or obsessive way. It is an enemy, and we need to see it for what it is and learn all we can about it:

> According to most scales of value, death is scarcely an estimable, worthwhile objective. It has far too many negative results to rate very high. It separates people, deprives one person of another, inflicts misery upon the least deserving, and dispenses an unremitting degree of evil. It is an enemy readily personified, even though it gets at us in many different ways, through injury, illness, catastrophe, failure, humiliation, and defeat.[2]

To be honest and educated in the ways of death; to know its motivations and goals; and to investigate, as much as possible, what lies beyond it may lessen the devastation of such a formidable foe and truly allow us to enjoy more of what life has to offer. As we understand death and deal with it appropriately, we keep ourselves from becoming enslaved to it. Consider these words from the book of Hebrews:

> He Himself [Jesus] likewise also partook of the same, that through death He might render powerless him who had the power of death, that is, the devil; and might deliver those who through fear of death were subject to slavery all their lives (Hebrews 2:14,15).

What a blessing that though we have to face death, as Christians we have been set free from being slaves to its gripping fear. But when we try to ignore death, we often fall into the trap of which Paul warns in Romans 6, making ourselves slaves to sin and death unnecessarily.

It is only natural for us to fear what we do not understand. That is why it is so important for us to courageously look at our enemy, knowing that death has been defeated, ultimately and finally.

Death Can Be Avoided

When death comes, a natural reaction is to try to prevent it from happening to you or to anyone else that you love. These words may sound familiar: "If you've got your health, you've got everything." Diet plans, health clubs, aerobics, nutrition, hiking, biking, swimming, and the beat goes on. Taking care of our bodies has become a national pastime.

Beneath all these good, virtuous activities lies a subtle message: As long as we stay healthy, we will live. As long as we live, we can avoid death. With enough exercise, the right food, and the proper precautions, we can put death on indefinite hold.

It is true that healthy people tend to live longer than unhealthy people. And certainly it is good to take care of our physical bodies. But all the health care in the world will not prevent death's visit when it is time. Being or becoming healthy should never become a substitute for dealing with the reality of death. Death has taken someone you love. And inevitably, death will come again.

Death Doesn't Matter

We live in an age when "just do it" and "do it now" have become our theme songs. And what about death? Well, that is relegated to the realm of "tomorrow." And tomorrow, frankly, doesn't matter. Because it is built squarely on the phantom foundation that "ignorance is bliss," this view of death has no room for God or His design for life. It is not difficult to see through this hopeless fiction, but it *is* difficult not to be taken in by the seemingly painless comfort it offers.

The truth in it is that today *is* important; it is valuable, and we should make the most of it. God made us to live and have fun and enjoy life. But making the most of today and truly enjoying life can only happen in light of the future.

When we get hooked by this fiction we find ourselves saying that we will deal with God and His life "later." We put God and reality on a back burner, relegating Him and His eternal truth to that which does not matter.

Jesus said that we ought to seek first His kingdom (His rule in our lives) and His righteousness (life as He designed it, including the reality of physical death) and He would take care of all those things that seem so important today (see Matthew 6:33).

Some years ago, Julius Haiduk, an Austrian school teacher, wrote a suicide note to his supervisor that illustrates the hopelessness of living without eternity in view:

> I beg of you, esteemed Herr Director, to receive kindly this, my last letter, even though it is written by a suicide, and to be charitable in judging this, my last act. I have expended all my energies to acquire broad knowledge and education. But, as a result, my feelings have become impoverished and all enjoyment of life has died in me. The endless routine of soulless teaching could not fill the emptiness in me. We form skillful technicians and argumentative pseudo-intellectuals but do not educate man for the true joy and divine virtue for which he was created. The new science which I have studied with such application has emptied the heavens of God, has despiritualized the world, and has degraded it to a mere soulless interaction of cogs in a dead mechanism. Such an existence is not worth living. Filled with disgust, I am withdrawing from it. Forgive me if by this auto-separation I am bringing sorrow to you and to my friends and wish me from the bottom of your heart the eternal rest I have eagerly desired for so long.[3]

> Yours,
> J.H.

Looking back on his life, Haiduk realized he had bought into the fiction that tomorrow does not matter, and all he was left with was despair.

There are many worldly voices in the choir of "understanding death." We hear them over and again, but we know they are a melody badly out of tune. Yet many people deny them outwardly while being infected by them inwardly. The problem is that the infection sometimes remains undiagnosed until the person is least prepared to face it—at the loss of someone near.

We can't become ostriches and put our heads in the sand, hoping that death will all go away. We need to take responsibility for our lives now and for knowing as much as we can about the very real possibility of life beyond the grave. As we discover the truth in our lives, we will be better able to face death honestly and courageously and without fear or denial. Being reminded of these voices can help us evaluate our own lives and in turn help someone else realize that Jesus has set us free from slavery to the fear of death. He came that we might truly live.

CHAPTER 9

The Freedom of Surrender

My people . . . have forsaken me,
the spring of living water,
and have dug their own cisterns,
broken cisterns that cannot hold water.

✦ Jeremiah 2:13

I THOUGHT I HAD a close relationship with the Lord, but when Kyle died I crumbled inside. I felt betrayed and robbed by the very One to whom I had always been so close. God had let me down. He had turned on me. Or at least that is what I believed at first. For years I pondered how I could ever have felt that way about my Father and Friend.

Now I know that I fell into such frustration not only because of my misconceptions and the impact of the worldly voices around me, but also because I had allowed myself to accept some images of the Lord that were not really the Lord Himself. In my search to understand death, I had to come to terms with my image of who God really is.

Sometimes we picture God as strong and powerful, like the *Godfather*. He can pull strings. He gets things done. He has a high degree of commitment to those who are absolutely loyal to him. But he is also very fickle with his love. And he can turn in a moment, from commitment to cruelty. He is a highly charged cannon, loose on the ship of life.

71

When we have this false image of God, we strive to be loyal to him, to get from him what he can give us that makes life a little better. But we also want to avoid his hair-trigger anger. We find ourselves thinking, "I'd better do everything just right. I don't want God mad at me. No telling what he might do to me or mine."

Consequently the loss of a loved one means we must have done something to rouse his displeasure. Death becomes his way of settling the score. If we picture God this way, we may feel that we have been unfairly judged, or that the judgment is far too severe. Our fury at this god can soar to new heights.

Superman is another way we can sometimes fallaciously view God. Like the Godfather, Superman is also very powerful. But unlike the Godfather, all of his motives and intentions are pure. He wants to do good, right the wrongs of the world, and spare people from pain and suffering. However, he does have some limitations. He cannot be everywhere at once. He tries to get around and keep on top of things as best he can, but he is a struggling hero . . . willing, but not able to get to it all.

If we have this view of God, we may think to ourselves, "I sure hope God is there when I need him," or, "I hope God can do something about this."

When we lose someone near we may be disappointed that this god was not present or powerful enough to save us from such a tragedy. We may begin to question the value of such a struggling hero. We may not exactly blame God, but we feel let down. The worth of God begins to decrease in our hearts. He is nice, but not to be counted on.

Then there is the *Heavenly Scorekeeper*. The Heavenly Scorekeeper is powerful, but for his own reasons he has chosen to be uninvolved in our lives. He created us and provided for us, and has now stepped back to keep score. There is no personal relationship with this false image.

Our role is to tally up as much good merit as possible in this life. We need to make sure we keep our "good" ahead of our "bad" because this god keeps an absolute and impartial score. When life is over he adds up the score and gives us what we deserve. This image of God produces thoughts such as "I hope my loved ones and I have been good enough for God."

But then we experience the death of someone near and discover that this is not a god we can call on. Suddenly all of our points mean nothing. This god is there, but unwilling to get involved. We may find ourselves angry at him for being able to save our loved one and our own pain, but not being willing to do so. We may also feel very alone in trying to deal with the trauma of loss. We will very likely question the morality and the worth of this god. Who wants to work so hard to spend eternity with a heartless scorekeeper?

There is yet another false image of God that pervades the Christian community. This is the *Genie in a Bottle*. The Genie in a Bottle is supernaturally powerful. He can do anything. And he is supposedly available at our beck and call. Just rub on the bottle by praying and the Genie suddenly appears, ready to grant our wishes. The Genie is under our control and is there only to fulfill our desires. This is a comfortable image of God in that he is never supposed to get in our way or out of our control. And his sole purpose is to grant us whatever we ask.

But then death stands before us. We call on our Genie to keep death from happening, or to remove the pain, or to help us get back to normal. There is no response. We call again and again, but to no avail. We may become enraged that our Genie is not following our wishes. We might think: "God has let me down. How dare he not respond when I call him!" We feel mad, helpless, and abandoned in our greatest time of need. The Genie is gone. God must have departed. We are left alone.

None of these false images of God can help us as we face the horror of loss through death. They are figments of our imaginations. They are not real. They are absolutely powerless to help us in any way at all. They are gods we have created in our own minds, in our own likeness. They are impotent impostors of the Almighty Lord. In the midst of our struggles they will all frustrate and abandon us.

We must examine our hearts. If we are following one of these false images of God, we need to turn back to the true Lord, the One who wants to give us life and joy and peace, even in the midst of sorrow and pain.

The one true God does not promise to take your pain away. Instead, He promises that in the midst of that pain, He will change your life. He will give you real life, a life in which you can experience true joy side-by-side with hurt and agony.

The Healing of Humility

I have never met a person yet who would openly admit to creating and following a false image of God. But our responses clearly show which god we are really following.

When Kyle died I called on my own false images of God for a while. But none could meet the challenge of my need. I became angry with their failure, dismayed by their lack of response, and I felt very much alone.

The only way to deal with the false images of God we create is to replace them with the true God. John 8:32 says, "You will know the truth, and the truth will set you free." The author to the Hebrews wrote that people should fix their eyes on Jesus, the Author and Finisher of their faith so that they would not grow weary and lose heart. Jesus, the true God, will not let you down but will keep you strong in your time of distress. That is what you need. Someone who will be there for you. A God who can and will make a difference.

Jesus is not at all like the false substitutes we make of Him. He is more powerful than all the powers of this world put together. And He loves you enough to have gone through a horrible, malicious death for you.

Paul wrote to the Philippians that Jesus humbled Himself and became obedient to the point of death—even the death of a cross:

> Therefore God exalted him to the highest place and gave him the name that is above every name, that at the name of Jesus every knee should bow, in heaven and on earth and under the earth, and every tongue confess that Jesus Christ is Lord, to the glory of God the Father (Philippians 2:9-11).

Those of us who have been sidetracked by our pain and sorrow and loneliness, and even anger, need to acknowledge once again that Jesus Christ is the Lord.

For me that meant I needed to go for some long walks in the woods. I had to spend time talking with my Lord and listening to his Word. It also meant taking time to be still, letting Him overwhelm me with the reality that He is God. He is the One who has everything under control. He is the One who has promised to give me the strength to go through any situation that comes into my life.

The struggle for me was that I was so caught up with "me" and "my agony" and "my loss" and "my anger" that I was not renewing my mind with the Lord's strength and presence and compassion and grace. I had not only run away from Judy and the kids with all my busyness, but like Jonah of old I had run away from the one true God. The only One who could really meet me at my point of need. But I hurt so badly, and found so little help anywhere else, that I quickly turned back to my Maker. I remember crying out to God: "Everything I am, and everything I have (including my wife and children) are

Yours." With those powerful words of emotion and deliberate choice, I finally surrendered my fighting will to my Lord.

Job was a biblical character who knew the secret of surrender. After he had gone through tremendous agony and grief, losing his family and all he held dear, he left us with this precious gem:

> I know that you can do all things; no plan of yours can be thwarted. [You asked,] "Who is this that obscures my counsel without knowledge?" Surely I spoke of things I did not understand, things too wonderful for me to know.
>
> [You said,] "Listen, now, and I will speak; I will question you, and you shall answer me." My ears had heard of you but now my eyes have seen you (Job 42:2-5).

Once Job got to the point where he could begin to see God for who He really was, something happened. Job says that his relationship with the Lord previously had all been on the surface: "My ears had heard of you." But now something was different. He says of this new relationship with his Lord: "Now my eyes have seen you."

It is as if Job is saying that before his torturous loss, he had only heard God on the radio or telephone. But now he saw God in living color. Job entered into a new, dynamic relationship with and appreciation for his Creator.

You and I may not have gone through the same depth of despair and loss as Job. But we can identify with his entering into a living relationship with his Lord. And we can deeply appreciate the difference it can make in the midst of our pain.

Bowing Before the Lord

Jesus Christ is the Lord of all. We cannot make Him into a god of our own choosing. We can only choose who we will be in relation to Him. We accept Him as our Master by coming to him in the same attitude of humility that He displayed.

Obviously, He is Lord no matter what we decide. But day by day we have a choice to make: We can humble ourselves before Him, or we can stubbornly lift our heads up and declare our independence from His rule in our lives. That is the heart of what James calls "pride." And "God opposes the proud but gives grace to the humble" (James 4:6).

Grace from God. Frankly, this is what we need in the face of grief and pain. We certainly do not need God's opposition to our selfish pride. Grace is reserved for the humble—for those willing to bow the knees of their heart before God and allow Him the absolute, unquestioned authority in their lives. James gives us this word of wisdom:

> Submit yourselves, then, to God. Resist the devil, and he will flee from you. Come near to God and he will come near to you. Wash your hands, you sinners, and purify your hearts, you double-minded. Grieve, mourn and wail. Change your laughter to mourning and your joy to gloom. Humble yourselves before the Lord, and he will lift you up (James 4:7-10).

In these verses we find four insights into living above the grief that has entered our lives:

"Submit to God....Resist the devil." To submit is to willingly give Jesus His designed and rightful place in every area of our lives. It is what Job did: the raising of the white flag in surrender as we lay down our fears, our anger, our frustrations, and our pain. We have to be willing to give up our "me" focus and our false images of God and surrender our wills to Him.

"Come near to God and he will come near to you." Drawing near to God demands taking time for Him. This is the

picture of the prodigal son finally returning home to his father. With his head held low, he sheepishly and slowly approached his father's house. He was fearful, I'm sure. Not certain how his father would react. But he was desperate. As he slunk toward his father, he was shocked to see his father running toward him with tears of joy and open arms of love. "Welcome back home, son!" he cried, as he embraced the son and kissed him. The father placed a ring on his son's finger and a robe over his rags and threw a celebration that must have totally blown the son's socks off—if he had any.

What a description for us. Draw near to God, says James, and He will draw near to you . . . arms wide open . . . ready to celebrate. Can I encourage you to take time for your Master? How can you possibly let Him be in control of your life if you are not listening to Him on a regular basis?

"Wash your hands, you sinners . . . change your laughter to mourning and your joy to gloom." We need to come to grips with the sin in our lives. Actually this sin is not too difficult to see. When we surrender our wills to our Lord and draw near to Him, the sin we have so cleverly disguised and denied rushes to the surface. We need only to admit what will become increasingly clear to us. And we need to see sin for the horror it really is. It will cause us grief. We will not quickly pass it off.

"But wait," you may be saying. "I'm already low enough! I don't need any more grief. I've done enough mourning and wailing already." The section finishes with one more insight:

"Humble yourselves before the Lord, and he will lift you up." When we bow our hearts before God, He will lift us up. As long as we stubbornly try to lift ourselves up and take care of ourselves, God will oppose our pride. The pain of loss will continue on . . . until we come back home where we belong, humbling ourselves before our Almighty Master.

Jesus says to each of us, "Come to me, all you who are weary and burdened, and I will give you rest. Take my yoke upon you and learn from me, for I am gentle and humble in heart, and you will find rest for you souls. For my yoke is easy and my burden is light" (Matthew 11:28-30).

God's grace is for those people who are willing to surrender to the Lord's design, even if it includes grief and sorrow. Then we will be lifted out of the mire of our grief. The pain will be overshadowed by the joy of being in a right relationship with our Master. The way up out of the pit of despair is down... down on our knees before the One who can lift us out and set us before His table of blessing.

> He lifted me out of the slimy pit, out of the mud and mire; he set my feet on a rock and gave me a firm place to stand (Psalm 40:2).

Chapter 10

Why Did He Have to Die?

What do you have against me? . . . Did you come to remind me of my sin and kill my son?

✦ Unknown widow to Elijah
(1 Kings 17:18)

NOT LONG AFTER KYLE'S DEATH, Bryan asked a simple, logical question that penetrated my theologically trained mind: "Why did Kyle die?"

Maybe you have asked that question. I know I have.

Tears came to my eyes as I realized I had nothing but a textbook response—an answer that seemed so inadequate in the face of such a profound question. "I'm sure that God has a million perfect purposes," I said. I believe that is a correct answer, but it seemed so utterly empty when the pangs of loss were so sharp.

Bryan's question helped motivate me to go back to God's Word to discover what it says about the purpose and process of death. I discovered that there is a rich and reasonable biblical response to the question, "Why did Kyle die?"

Here's some of what I've learned about why there is such a thing as hard and tragic as death . . . beginning with the foundations of death.

The Beginning

"In the beginning God created the heavens and the earth" (Genesis 1:1). In less time than it took for you to read that familiar verse, God our Creator brought time and space, our universe, into existence. He created something completely new.

Part of what God created was mankind. "God said, 'Let us make man in our image, in our likeness'" (Genesis 1:26). God created all other living creatures after their own kind, but mankind was different. God created us after *His* image.

We were given a special dignity and worth far beyond all the other living creatures of God's creation. Man's aliveness was from the very breath, or Spirit, of God. Physically, man was made from the dust of the ground. But when God breathed His Spirit into man, giving that physical clay life, we became living souls with individual personalities (Genesis 2:7).

How crucial it is to remember that life is a marvelous, wondrous gift from God. You and I did nothing at all to deserve life, nor to enjoy the gift of someone else's life.

The Choice

But God gave mankind even more than life. He wanted to have an intimate relationship with those He created in His own likeness. By definition, meaningful relationships must be mutually chosen. God chose to relate to Adam and Eve, but how did they respond?

> And the Lord God commanded the man, "You are free to eat from any tree in the garden; but you must not eat from the tree of the knowledge of good and evil" (Genesis 2:16,17).

Adam and Eve had a very real choice presented to them. The choice they made would directly affect them and their relationship with their Father. And, in fact, it would affect all mankind from that time on.

God continues to give people the freedom and ability to make very real choices. Of course there are areas over which we have no control. We cannot choose to eliminate God or change what God calls good into something inherently bad. But we can make important choices in areas like love, obedience, faith, hope, faithfulness, and communication. Our most important choice is whether or not we are going to follow God's design for living in relationship with Him. This choice is so significant because everything else in our lives is affected by our response. And it not only affects our lives now, but for all eternity.

Some people ask, "Why did God make the choice and consequences so severe? Why didn't He just let Adam and Eve, and through them the rest of mankind, choose between the tree of *good* and the tree of *very good*? Why are the consequences so extreme?"

God did not want a mediocre relationship with His special creations. He wanted the deepest relationship possible. That requires very meaningful choices on man's part. And heavy rewards and consequences that go with those choices.

What does all this say about God's opinion of you and me? It clearly shows that God places a high value on His relationship with us. It also implies that He has made us with the substance and maturity to be able to make choices with lasting ramifications.

When my children were very young they saw my watch and, one by one, began to ask for a watch of their own. Although limited finances had something to do with it, I did not buy them watches of the same value as my own. Why? Because my children are not as important or valuable as I am? Of course not! They simply weren't mature enough to handle the kinds of responsibilities that go along with a finely crafted watch. As they have grown older and more capable of handling those kinds of responsibilities, I have given them proportionately better watches.

So it is with us and God. He created us to be able to handle the kind of responsibility that goes along with living in a dynamic relationship with Him. He has entrusted us with the responsibility of choices and their consequences. He thinks very highly of us.

The Impact

> And the Lord God commanded the man, "You are free to eat from any tree in the garden; but you must not eat from the tree of the knowledge of good and evil, for when you eat of it you will surely die" (Genesis 2:16,17).

Man and woman ate. In doing so they thought they were choosing a more godlike life than they already had. In reality that was impossible. They were already created in the likeness of God. Their choice was shattering. When they followed the advice of Satan, who had given them nothing and promised them what was not in their best interest, they chose to despise God's gift of life and relationship. They made the choice to be unfaithful to their faithful Creator.

That frightful choice carried a weighty price tag. As wondrous and magnificent as the blessing of a dynamic, living relationship with God was, so also was the horror and unimaginable pain of the curse with its separation from intimate relationship with their Father and Creator.

The prophet Isaiah said, "Behold, the Lord's hand is not so short that it cannot save; neither is His ear so dull that it cannot hear. *But your iniquities have made a separation between you and your God*" (Isaiah 59:1,2 NASB, *emphasis added*). The horror of the curse is that human beings chose a direction in life that built a wall of separation between them and their Creator. When God came looking for Adam and Eve to walk with them in the garden in the cool of the day, they hid.

God called to man. Man responded that he was afraid. Fear had been born in mankind—fear to stand face-to-face with the Creator. Man made a choice that changed his ability to relate with God the way his Designer had wanted and made possible.

I love my children passionately. Along with Judy they are my closest friends in all the world. I love being their dad! But there are times when one of my children makes an unfortunate choice that changes them and makes it impossible for us to share the deep, meaningful relationship we had previously enjoyed. At these times, my heart yearns to get back to the relationship we had before. I long for what we can have and have had together. But what we did have was based on a *mutual* relationship.

With the passion of a loving Father, God longs for us to be able to have that binding, loving communion that He intended. But it takes two for that kind of relationship. God hasn't changed—we have. This miserable rift between us and our Father is at the heart of the curse.

The Father's Promise

Mankind was helpless to get back into a deep, meaningful relationship with his Creator. The knowledge of good and evil was more than we were designed to handle, and it had become part of the fabric of our being. We could not eradicate that which had changed us and our ability to relate with God. Yet God did not leave us without hope. That hope came in the person of Jesus Christ, God's Son. Jesus came to mend the rift in our relationship with our heavenly Father. Paul explained this when he wrote:

> Therefore, there is now no condemnation for those who are in Christ Jesus, because through Christ Jesus the law of the Spirit of life set me free from the law of sin and death. For

what the law was powerless to do in that it was
weakened by the sinful nature, God did by
sending his own Son in the likeness of sinful
man to be a sin offering. And so he condemned
sin in sinful man, in order that the righteous
requirements of the law might be fully met in
us (Romans 8:1-4).

Adam and Eve's tragic choice has been dealt with once
and for all. All sins—past, present and future—have
been accounted for and cleared (1 John 2:2). Through His
death Jesus Christ has saved us from having to live
eternally separated from our Father. He has opened the
door for restoration to begin. That is a magnificent truth,
and a costly one to both our Father and His Son.

God continues to desire a mutual relationship with
you and me. But how do we enter into it? John explains:

Yet to all who received Him, to those who
believed in his name, He gave the right to
become children of God—children born not of
natural descent, nor of human decision or a
husband's will, but born of God (John 1:12,13).

We simply have to receive His gift. What an amazing
God. He does all the work. He pays the price for the
shambles we have created. All He asks us to do to restore
our relationship is to accept His gift of life through Christ.

People respond in varying fashions to the claims of
Christ. Some do not take them seriously, while others
feel they were simply an act to gain people's attention.
Some say Jesus was a great teacher; others a great prophet,
but nothing more. To these kinds of responses, C.S.
Lewis remarked:

I am trying here to prevent anyone saying
the really foolish thing that people often say

about Him: "I'm ready to accept Jesus as a great moral teacher, but I don't accept His claim to be God." That is one thing we must not say. A man who was merely a man and said what Jesus said would not be a great moral teacher. He would either be a lunatic—on a level with the man who says he is a poached egg—or else he would be the Devil of Hell. You must make your choice. Either this man was, and is, the Son of God: or else a madman or something worse. You can shut Him up for a fool, you can spit at Him and kill Him as a demon; or else you can fall at His feet and call Him Lord and God. But let us not come with any patronizing nonsense about His being a great human teacher. He has not left that open to us. He did not intend to.[1]

Each of us must make our own choice to receive Jesus Christ as God's gift to heal our broken relationship. We must each live, and die, with our choice.

The Blessing

So why did Kyle have to die?

For the same reason as Adam and Eve. They were separated from God (spiritually dead) as soon as they ate from the tree. They were changed people, and so was their relationship with God.

But why did Adam die *physically*? Why not let Adam live? God responded to that alternative by saying:

> The man has now become like one of us, knowing good and evil. He must not be allowed to reach out his hand and take also from the tree of life and eat, and live forever (Genesis 3:22).

What would have happened had Adam and Eve eaten from the tree of life? They would never have died physically. But they would have lived on eternally with sin being part of the fabric of their being. The kind of close, intimate relationship that God wanted and still wants us to enjoy would have been eternally impossible.

From an eternal perspective, then, physical death is a blessing. Our loving Father is willing to let us face the hard and horrifying reality of physical death so that we can have something far outweighing the painful loss: eternity with Him, in His home, without any walls of separation between us—forever. Paul reminds us in Romans 8 that our present suffering cannot even begin to compare the eternal glory waiting for God's children.

Why did Kyle die? He died because of sin. He died so he can live with His Father, closely, intimately, securely forever. That is our Father's promise. What a great place for Kyle to be.

CHAPTER 11

Why Does It Hurt So Much?

Yet for the mourners it is as though life has stopped within.
As mourners we feel that we too have died; death moves in
to occupy and posses us, to join with us and be part of us.

✦ Joan Hagen Arnold and
Penelope Buschman Geema

OFTEN IN THE MONTHS FOLLOWING Kyle's drowning, Judy and I would find ourselves sitting on the couch crying together. We did not even have to be talking about Kyle. The tears just flowed.

Several times, either Bryan or Eric would come in from outside, put their arms around our necks, and ask, "Are you missing Kyle again?" "Yes, we are," we would reply. "We are really missing Kyle right now. Thanks for the hug. That helps."

We were missing Kyle again . . . and again. It hurt so badly. But why? That was a question Judy and I asked ourselves many times. We were tired of hurting. We were tired of crying. But we found it hard to handle the hurt honestly.

At times we would try to deny the pain, and tell other people we were just fine—we wanted to be anyway. And then we would find ourselves back on that couch, tears springing from our hearts once again.

Over the years I have learned much about death. I have learned that it was not part of God's original design, nor His future plans. It is a consequence of the choice made by Adam—and each of us. But while I had already learned much about death, I still did not know the true answer to the question my heart kept asking: What *is* death? My investigation into the truth about death proved to be one of the most difficult explorations of my life, and one of the most valuable.

The following is some of what I discovered in the Bible. It gives quite a picture of death—from several angles—and has helped me to understand exactly why it hurts so badly.

Scripture uses the word "death" to illustrate the physical decline of the body; the cessation of our existence; and the separation of the body from the spirit, of man from God, and of one person from another. Once I saw death for what it really is, I realized that it *should* hurt. In fact, it made me wonder about those who say it does not hurt.

Ashes to Ashes; Dust to Dust

Our physical bodies came from the dust of the ground, and they will return to dust. The Bible often uses the word "death" to speak of the demise of our physical body. Our bodies wear out. They are susceptible to deterioration, diseases, and destruction. We call the result death. Moses painted a graphic picture of death in Psalm 90. He and the newly formed nation of Israel were wandering in the wilderness. They were not lost. They were waiting. Waiting for an entire generation of people— millions of them—who had sinned against God to die. Waiting so a new generation would be able to enter the promised land.

Moses lamented the death of those people. He had been their leader. And now he was watching them die, one by one. But Moses knew that God was the final authority:

Lord, you have been our dwelling place throughout all generations. Before the mountains were born or you brought forth the earth and the world, from everlasting to everlasting you are God. You turn men back to dust, saying, "Return to dust, O sons of men." For a thousand years in your sight are like a day that has just gone by, or like a watch in the night. You sweep men away in the sleep of death; they are like the new grass of the morning—though in the morning it springs up new, by evening it is dry and withered. We are consumed by your anger and terrified by your indignation. You have set our iniquities before you, our secret sins in the light of your presence. All our days pass away under your wrath; we finish our years with a moan. The length of our days is seventy years—or eighty, if we have the strength; yet their span is but trouble and sorrow, for they quickly pass, and we fly away (Psalm 90:1-10).

Moses spoke of death as returning to the dust, as falling asleep, as grass that sprouts, flourishes, fades, and withers. He says our days have declined and finished with a sigh and that our life may contain 70 or 80 years, but soon they are gone and we fly away.

My grandmother, whom we called "Mama Head," lived with my family off and on for more than 20 years. As Mama Head lived into her later eighties, and then into her middle nineties, her physical body kept wearing down. I saw her finishing her years "with a moan." Slowly but surely death was taking my grandmother's life away from her. She became forgetful. It was painful to walk. It hurt to sit too long, walk too long, or lie down for too long. Her physical body was grinding to a halt.

It hurt me to see Mama Head wearing down. She had always been so alive, so vital, so rich in history and wisdom and love. Death was taking all those wonderful gifts from her.

I do not remember when it was exactly, but I do remember that there came a point when I realized my grandmother really was going to die someday. Her continued physical decline left me with no other conclusion. Our physical bodies do not live indefinitely on their own. They stop. Dust returns to dust. That is a painful reality. It hurts to experience it and to see someone you love going through it.

The Ending of "Aliveness"

The word "death" is also used in Scripture to signify the ending of "life." The picture here is not of the physical body, but the time when the aliveness of a person ceases to exist.

The "aliveness" of ones we love deeply affects us. Our loved ones add winks and whistles and whispers to our experience. They inspire and enrich our lives with their vitality. When someone who is an integral part in our life dies, a chapter in the book of our life is closed.

Each August on Kyle's birthday Judy pulls out the family album we made when he was alive. We all take time, either alone or together, to wander through the pictures with their images of Kyle laughing, playing, being. We sit there and experience life as it was then. We will hear the laughs, feel the hugs and kisses, agonize over the hurts and settle the disputes between brothers.

Each year at this time I am reminded again that Kyle was a crucial part of the aliveness of each member of the Taylor family. When he died, Judy lost her helper and chief assistant and her first student. Bryan and Eric lost their leader. They had never experienced life without their older brother. Much of their world was tightly wrapped around his presence. For years we had each molded and adapted our lives around Kyle. In a moment that life was gone. His presence, his aliveness had ceased to exist in the way we had always known it.

Friends at the camp and at school, teachers at church and at school, family and friends in other parts of the world—all had been affected by Kyle's life. His aliveness was no longer available. It was gone.

The pictures remind us of Kyle and the life we shared. When we put the album down and look at the present picture of our family, there is something missing. Our minds ask, "What's wrong with this picture?" Our hearts quickly respond, "Kyle is missing. That's what." And with him hopes and dreams and plans and promises. Not only was the past cut short, but so was the future we had imagined. Each of us was robbed of Kyle's life. That which was so vitally a part of our lives, and our thoughts for the future, no longer existed. It was gone, never to return.

Separation

The Bible also speaks of death as a "separation." This concept is presented in many different ways, making it crucial to understand what separation means, and what it does not mean. Separation is not a convenient, painless breaking apart. It is not merely uncomfortable. It is the tearing apart of something that was previously united or of one piece.

In the early 1940s the Nazi regime established its infamous concentration camps for containing and exterminating anyone considered undesirable. When people stepped off the overcrowded, unsanitary cattle cars, they were greeted by the unforgettable stench of burning flesh. They were quickly herded by Nazi guards into single-file lines to wait their turn to face the Nazi official at the front. As people came to the front of the line, he would motion either to his left or his right. Guards stood ready to take these weary people to their fate.

No signs told them what lay ahead. Families would come to the official, holding tightly to each other, wanting only to go together—whatever their fate.

But it was not to be. The official would point one way for the father and another for the daughter he was holding. One guard would step forward and tear the young girl from his arms. Another guard would seize him and drag him the other way. The father was helpless to save his daughter. He could not go with her. They would scream and reach and beg and plead. But to no avail.

Then a mother and baby would face the official, to be separated—ripped apart.

That is what death is. Separation. A tearing apart of that which is united and one. We are hurt by death because it tears apart something good and right, something natural and normal, without respect to families or friends.

Separation of the Body and Spirit

A few years ago I had the privilege of performing a Christmas Eve wedding for two friends, Jeff and Debbie. They loved each other dearly. Six months later Jeff suffered a massive heart attack in the middle of the night. He never woke up. I found myself overseeing his memorial service a few days later, and as I stood above the casket, looking down, I saw the shell of the vital, energetic man I had known.

I kept expecting Jeff to give me that familiar wink and sit up. I could almost hear him speak and laugh and cry. But Jeff's spirit had left his body. There was no living personality inside that casket. His body and his soul had been torn apart. He and Debbie had been torn apart. He and I had been torn apart. Death ripped Jeff's spirit from his body, leaving an empty shell.

In Genesis 2, God formed man out of the dust of the earth. He breathed into that physical body His Spirit which gave the body a living soul. God's Spirit energized the physical body so that it took on a unique personality—the expression of aliveness through the mind, emotions, and will of the man.

At death that body and spirit are separated—torn apart. The body is left as it began ... dust.

Separation from God

In an earlier chapter we looked carefully at the separation between us and our Creator Father. God designed us to be able to share mutually in a deep, vital, meaningful relationship with Him. But our sin, through Adam and Eve, tore apart that relationship—that walking together in the garden in the cool of the evening.

This separation took place because mankind desired to strike out and try to establish a life of his own without dependence on God. The Bible tells us that there is a way of living that seems right to a man, but its end is the way of death (Proverbs 14:12).

The separation of man and his God is an unmistakable form of death. Physical death around us is a constant reminder of this way of separation that we have chosen. It is also a reminder that even though we want to and try desperately to control life—we cannot!

Separation from the Land of the Living

Some passages in the Old Testament depict death as a "tearing away" of a person from those who are still living—from family and friends. For example, Isaiah 53:8 predicts that the promised Messiah will be *"cut off from the land of the living."* This is very similar to the "ending of aliveness" that we noted earlier, but the emphasis in separation is on the *tearing away* that happens. Sometimes this is anticipated; for example, by a mother who knows she is dying and leaving a husband and young children. But it is felt just as keenly by those whose loved one dies suddenly, unexpectedly. The one who has died has not only ceased to live; there is a sense in which he has been ripped away.

After Kyle's memorial service, and occasionally for a few more years, Bryan and Eric asked, "Where is Kyle now? Is he still in the water? Is he in the ground? Is he in heaven with God?" They were very young, and it was difficult for them to adjust to the fact that Kyle was permanently gone. Separated from them. They wanted to know where he was. They felt his absence from their lives keenly.

Often the pain that comes from this "tearing away" makes other people uncomfortable. They do not know what to do or say. Death has changed their lives too. They may hurt for us, but they feel helpless. So they often say nothing, avoiding the subject at all costs. Not understanding this pain that separation has brought, they seek to handle death the best way they can: by pushing it as far from their thoughts as possible in an attempt to escape the reality that death has ripped away a loved one from those of us who are still alive.

Why does death hurt so badly? Because it is destruction and separation. Death rips apart the body from the spirit, husbands from wives, parents from children, families from friends.

Judy and I sat on the couch and cried. Sure we did. We agonized the tearing away of Kyle's life from our family and the land of the living.

✦ ✦ ✦

"Are you missing Kyle again?"
Of course. Separation hurts.

Learning to Live Again

God isn't in the business of giving lighter loads, but of stepping in with us, giving us stronger backs.

—Author unknown

CHAPTER 12

Joy Is a Choice

I may go so far as to say that you may not be able to have a lifestyle of joy without knowing pain in some intimate way.

◆ Tim Hansel

THE LOSS OF SOMEONE NEAR captures our attention, and that is only as it should be. In a moment of time, life has been changed forever. And the closer we were to the one who has gone on without us, the deeper the hurt and the pain. The wound left by death is severe.

A friend once asked, "When does it go away? When does the overwhelming pain stop?" Getting the weight of pain off our shoulders can become the preoccupation of our lives. But, unfortunately, the harder we try to get rid of it, the worse it becomes.

You will not find a formula in this book for ridding yourself of pain. I would have to deny the ache that still lingers after all these years to convince you that the pain can or will go away. Rather, learning how to live life fully after someone you love is gone starts by realizing and admitting that pain continues. Pain is not the enemy of living. What makes pain good or bad is the intention of the one inflicting or allowing the pain.

When I was young my parents would not allow me to play ball on the only big, flat area in our neighborhood— the busy street in front of our home. More than once my dad subjected me to physical pain over this rule, and because of the spankings I finally decided not to play in the street. I would sometimes sit on the curb in utter frustration that two people could be so unfair and mean. I tried my best to figure out ways to get around the rule. I even prayed that God would bring my parents to their senses and change the rule so I could do what I wanted. But all my wishes and schemes and prayers were to no avail.

Was my internal and external pain bad? No, neither my parents nor God answered my wishes because it was not in my best interest. It was far better for me to suffer in a mild fashion so that I could live to grow up. Pain can be used for good or evil, depending on the motive of the one behind it.

Death and separation cause a great deal of pain. God allows us to hurt over the loss of someone near, but for good reason. God wants to change my life and yours. He wants us to be more complete, more of who he designed us to be, more of the people we so passionately long to be deep inside. Throughout this closing section we will look at ways the Father wants to help us learn to live again. As we grow in our understanding of the true nature of joy, as we open our hearts to the love that still waits to be given and received, as we sense the help of God's Spirit, and as we set our priorities with eternity in view, God will use the pain we are experiencing to bring us to a place where we can live the "changed life" *joyously*.

Pain and Joy Go Together

In my struggle over the loss of Kyle, I have found much strength and direction and encouragement in the book of James. James, the half-brother of Jesus and senior pastor at the church of Jerusalem, wrote these words to his dispersed, hurting congregation: "Consider it pure joy, my brothers, whenever you face trials of many kinds" (James 1:2).

As James' letter unfolds, it is clear that his readers were indeed facing many and varied trials: prejudice, doubt, gossip and slander, hypocrisy, unfair treatment by the rich, favoritism toward those with power, and disregard for the poor. The word that James uses for trials refers to potholes in the path of life: those un-expected, unforeseen, undesirable road hazards that throw us off course and make us lose our balance. James goes so far as to say that the trials in life are "many." There are more of them than we can count or imagine, and they come in a multitude of sizes, shapes, and col-ors. Facing the death of someone we care deeply about is one of the major trials we encounter in life.

A most remarkable phrase in these words from James is the simple word "whenever." He does not say "if," but "whenever" we face these potholes. Pain and suffering are a part of life. Not *if*, but *when*. Each of us who has lost someone near needs to realize that pain is not the enemy of life; rather it is a primary means God uses to help us discover a more complete, fulfilling way of living.

Choosing Joy

Kyle's death was totally unforeseen. When it came it seemed more like the Grand Canyon than a pothole to me. Never in my life would I have thought Kyle's time on earth would last for only 5½ years. That is why the words "Kyle is dead!" blindsided me.

My joy fled when Kyle was gone. But James says, "Consider it pure joy, my brothers, whenever you face trials of many kinds." Joy? With Kyle dead and my heart broken? How could I ever be joyful again? It didn't make any sense at all. Surely James was out of touch with reality. But just the opposite was true. James understood a truth that I needed desperately to understand—pain and joy can coexist. In fact, they go hand-in-hand in this life.

Up to this time I would have been more likely to define joy as the lack of pain, not something that goes hand-in-glove with it. They were on opposite teams, not working together. How can these two apparent opposites be reconciled?

When we use the word "consider" today, we usually mean "to think about" or "regard" something. But when James says to "consider it pure joy," he means to *account* it as joy. Joy is a choice. It is a function of the mind rather than the heart.

Joy is the emotion you experience when you have been set free. It is the lifting up of your souls in the midst of pain. It is far more than just being happy; it is the excitement that comes with being liberated. It is the enthusiastic spirit that results from receiving an unexpectedly pleasant surprise.

A few weeks ago Judy, who teaches part-time in a local elementary school, was going through a very difficult time. Another teacher, a friend of hers, had died unexpectedly of a heart attack in the night. Because of her background, Judy was able to help the children begin to understand and deal with their pain, but I could sense her energy wearing thin. She began doubting herself.

One day I had a small vase of flowers delivered to her classroom with the simple note, "I'm proud of you, and I love you." When the secretary entered her room and brought her the flowers, Judy was touched. This small, unexpected surprise lifted her above the pain around her and in her own heart. The pain did not leave. But neither was it allowed to drag her down any further. Something had been added to her life that made the pain bearable. That something brought joy to her.

James doesn't say that we should experience joy "because of" the painful trials we are going through. Rather, he says, we need to use every opportunity to experience pure joy because our Father is sending us something, special delivery, that will set us free from pain's downward pull. We need to have the eyes of our heart open so that we don't miss His surprises.

Special Delivery

What is the gift sent from God that can bring us joy in the midst of our pain? James says, "You know that the testing of your faith develops perseverance" (James 1:3). God is in the process of using trials—the pain of our loss—to test our faith and produce perseverance in our lives.

When James says that God is testing our faith, he is not saying that God is grading us to see how well we do. Rather he is saying something that Peter also illustrates in 1 Peter 1:6,7:

> In this you greatly rejoice, though now for a little while you may have had to suffer grief in all kinds of trials. These have come so that your faith—of greater worth than gold, which perishes even though refined [tested] by fire—may be proved genuine and may result in praise, glory and honor when Jesus Christ is revealed.

The context here, as in James, is "all kinds of trials." Peter says that God will use these trials to test our faith. But then he explains the goal of this kind of testing: to produce in us the kind of life that brings praise and glory and honor to the Lord.

Gold is tested by putting fire to it, which purifies and strengthens the metal. It gets out all the impurities and leaves the metal more solid and more durable. That is what God does with our faith: He strengthens and purifies it. Knowing this gave me little comfort at first. My pain overwhelmed me. I could not grasp the joy. But finally after many months I began to understand.

God wants to bless us. Do you believe that? I didn't. I said the words, but I never really believed them. We have a perfect Father who knows how to give us the greatest possible joy in our lives. And He is willing to help us, even when we don't enjoy or appreciate what He is doing in our lives. True joy and blessing and fulfillment for each of us is found as we live through the difficulties in a trusting, dependent, "solid gold" relationship with God.

It is because we *know* that God will bring us through the difficult times that we can experience pure joy in the midst of tremendous pain. That is at the heart of God's plan. No matter how much we may hurt over the loss of someone near, we can be free to experience joy.

I still miss my son's presence and aliveness with our family. Dealing with the loss of our father-son relationship has proved to be a difficult journey. But going through that process has brought me so much closer in my Father-son relationship with my heavenly Father. As I've come to know the Father better, and as our relationship has become more alive and intimate, I've come to enjoy my wife, my family, and my own aliveness in a richer, fuller way.

Many people think that if they can accumulate enough things and avoid enough pain, they will experience joy. But that is not how it works. Only as we learn to live in faith, in a relationship built on trust and dependence on God, are we able to experience *His* joy and blessing. Only then can we discover all that He has designed us to be. God knows that. He wanted me to know it too.

I knew it in my head, but I had not put it into practice in my life on a daily basis. I simply had not given it enough time to sink into my heart. The more I understood that truth, the more God was, and is, able to be all He wants to be in my life.

One of the many things God wanted to do for me was to give me a greater freedom in the expression of my personality. I now laugh more, cry more, love more, and feel more anger when I see injustice. I am freer to live without worrying about the "what if's" and the "what might have been's" that used to stifle me. I have a greater-than-ever sense that God really is in charge. And when new circumstances come into my life unexpectedly, instead of being overwhelmed, I know that God has a way to help me through every one of them.

Joy Comes with Growth

Another way God wants to help us live life to the fullest is to make us more durable. Instead of lightening our load, He wants to help us carry heavier loads. We wish and pray that God would take the difficulties away, but He wants us to be able to take on more, and do it victoriously as we learn to cast our cares on Him and become partners with Him in life.

Perseverance is the word James uses. It is also translated "endurance"—the ability to keep going even when faced with seemingly insurmountable odds.

I used to be a runner of sorts. There was a time in life when I ran five to ten miles most mornings. It took one painfully stretching day after another to build up my endurance, but in time running became a joy. I felt I could run forever. I was happy that I had persevered through the earlier pain and developed the endurance I had. Somehow the pain of the training paled in comparison to the joy of the run. And so it is with life as God designed it.

There is a deep-seated part of us that is convinced that the key to fulfillment is avoiding discomfort. What a sorrow that must be to our Father. He wants us to stop living a false and dangerous illusion. He wants us to grow up and to mature. He wants us to be able to persevere in real life. Joy comes with growing up.

So how is it possible to persevere and grow through death and loss? What do we need to do to recognize and appreciate God's ability to lift us above the mire of pain?

Simply stated, the bottom line is faith. But faith is one of those Christian words that is so familiar that it is in danger of becoming a cliché. To some people, faith is a blind leap into the unknown. It is hoping against all hope because we do not know what else to do. This kind of faith is empty. It is hollow and will never help us find real life in the midst of our struggle with loss. It will fail and frustrate us. We will grow to despise it. This is not biblical faith.

To other people, faith is just wishful thinking. It is wanting something to be true so much that we imagine it to be so. We think that if we wish for something long enough, we can make it happen. But if we view faith this way, we are setting ourselves up for a fall. In the end, it will only add to our hurt. Wishful thinking is not biblical faith either.

Neither of these misconceptions of true faith will help us find life. Biblical faith has a different foundation. It is built on trust in God. But faith takes more than trust. It requires courage as well—the willingness to take risks in the face of perceived danger. Trusting God is not easy. It does not come naturally to us.

On that cool, rainy morning in April, Kyle had the courage to risk his life in the hope of saving his frantic, struggling younger brother. For months I tried to insulate myself from the unmerciful pain of losing my son. At times I wanted to die so I could get out of that horrid pit of despair. Only God knew the depth of my torment, my self-pity, my unwillingness to face the reality of Kyle's death.

Then one day Judy mentioned that Kyle had lived up to his biblical namesake, Daniel. Like this Bible hero, Kyle had marched bravely into his personal lion's den. Kyle Daniel Taylor's last act was one of monumental courage and risk in the face of incredible danger. He risked his life to save Eric. My heart warmed with gratitude for having had such a brave son. He was such a courageous young man!

Kyle was willing to give his life for what he believed was right, while I was afraid to face my own pain and grief and heartache. Kyle's act of courage slapped the face of my tentativeness. It caught my attention.

God has graciously used Kyle's life, and yes, his death, to teach me something about the courage to trust God.

With Kyle's death I found myself in an unmapped wilderness. I knew who to trust, but did I have the courage to trust Him? Could I show the same courage to face my new life that Kyle had as he faced his death?

In the days of Moses the people also had to make a choice. Did they have the courage to trust God, or were they going to cling to what was inadequate, detestable, but familiar? Let's look closely at this famous battle on the field of faith.

> The Lord said to Moses, "Send some men to explore the land of Canaan, which I am giving to the Israelites. . . ."
> When Moses sent them to explore Canaan, he said, "Go up through the Negev and on into the hill country. See what the land is like and whether the people who live there are strong or weak, few or many" (Numbers 13:1,2,17,18).

The Lord wanted the Israelites to go see and hear and smell the land He was giving to them, their new home. So Moses sent leaders out to explore the land and its people. There must have been a wave of excitement in the air as these explorers left on their journey. I'm sure there was a buzz around camp while they were gone. And surely men were posted to let Moses and the others know when the heroes returned to camp. Finally the day of their return arrived:

They gave Moses this account: "We went into the land to which you sent us, and it does flow with milk and honey! Here is its fruit. But the people who live there are powerful, and the cities are fortified and very large. We even saw descendants of Anak there. The Amalekites live in the Negev; the Hittites, Jebusites and Amorites live in the hill country; and the Canaanites live near the sea and along the Jordan" (Numbers 13:27-29).

What a land they saw. Flowing with milk and honey. Giant fruit, sweet and plump. But the people! The fortified cities! The huge crowds began to hiss and mumble. They did not expect this kind of a report. As the murmuring spread, the volume began to drown out the spies.

Then Caleb silenced the people before Moses and said, "We should go up and take possession of the land, for we can certainly do it." But the men who had gone up with him said, "We can't attack those people; they are stronger than we are" (Numbers 13:30,31).

The stage was set for a showdown. Caleb, one of the spies, wanted to pack up right then and take the land that God was giving them. But 10 of the 12 spies, the overwhelming majority, said, "Impossible! They are too strong." Caleb shouted, "We can certainly do it." The ten retorted, "We can't."

That night all the people of the community raised their voices and wept aloud. All the Israelites grumbled against Moses and Aaron, and the whole assembly said to them, "If only we had died in Egypt! Or in this desert! Why is the Lord bringing us to this land only to let us fall by the sword? Our wives and children will be taken as plunder. Wouldn't it be better for us to go back to Egypt?" And they said to each other, "We should choose a leader and go back to Egypt" (Numbers 14:1-4).

The people of the community had a choice to make. Just one.

That choice was not really over whether they should take the land or not. It was not over whether to go back to Egypt or stay where they were at. It had nothing to do with their wives or children, or whether to replace their leader. None of these was the real choice facing the people that long, restless night in the Israelite camp.

They simply had to decide whether they were going to trust God or not. God had already told them that He was giving them this land. All they had to do was go up and accept His gift. Did they trust that God would do it? That He *could* do it?

The people tipped their hand ahead of time by the way they started grasping for other straws to save themselves from this unexpected change in life. There were options. They could go back to Egypt or get another human leader. But which of these alternatives could possibly help them in the distress brought on by unexpected changes in their lives?

We are faced with the same choice. God promises us a good land, a land flowing with milk and honey beyond the wilderness we are in. But all too often we behave just like the Israelites who turned their backs on God, grumbling as they turned, and looked for other worthless, empty things to trust in.

Are you willing to trust God when He says you should persevere through your pain? When He says that He will enable you to become a more complete person on the other side? Are you willing to accept pain as part of life, trusting God to lift you up, just as He promises?

CHAPTER 13

The Heart
of Trust

I waited patiently for the Lord;
*   he turned to me and heard my cry.*
He lifted me out of the slimy pit,
*   out of the mud and mire;*
he set my feet on a rock
*   and gave me a firm place to stand.*
Blessed is the man
*   who makes the Lord his trust. . . .*

✦ Psalm 40:1,2,4

WHY DID SOME of the Israelites trust God, while others chose not to? Why, for instance, were Joshua and Caleb willing to stand up to the other spies and encourage the people to take the bountiful land that God had said He would give them? Listen to these words of God about Caleb:

> But because my servant Caleb has a different spirit and follows me wholeheartedly, I will bring him into the land he went to, and his descendants will inherit it (Numbers 14:24).

Caleb was God's servant. He had a "different spirit." He followed his Lord wholeheartedly. Because Caleb had humbled his heart before the Lord and become His bondservant, he was special. He was ready, willing, and able to follow His Lord wholeheartedly, doing whatever He said.

Caleb wanted to trust God for the biggest city, with the biggest walls, on the biggest hill, filled with the biggest people. One could truly see why Caleb was recognized as having a different spirit, a spirit not of timidity but of *courage*. Courage comes with being a bondservant of Jesus Christ.

There is something very interesting about this kind of courage. It anticipates the next time it can be called upon. It finds the most refreshment and vitality when it is in the thick of things.

I have found this to be true in my own life since Kyle's death. I do not look forward to the problems that come my way as a pastor of a growing church. But when they come I know that I will not have to face them alone. God is there with me, helping me, consoling me, stretching me, and strengthening me. He will help me see where I need to change, and He will give me the strength to face whatever situations arise. Wherever you are in your life, God has plans for you, too. We have been "created in Christ Jesus to do good works, which God prepared in advance for us to do" (Ephesians 2:10). God will give you the strength to accomplish everything He has planned for you.

How Do I Trust?

At this point I had to ask myself another question: If courage to trust God is necessary for me to live for Christ wholeheartedly, and becoming a bondservant is necessary for me to have a courageous "different spirit," then what is the key to becoming such a bondservant?

The answer is not complex or even particularly hard to grasp. In fact, the answer is very simple. But it is far from easy! It is not difficult because of what we have to do, but because of what we have to *stop* doing. What we have to give up.

The apostle Paul understood this truth. A Pharisee among Pharisees, Paul followed all the right rules, knew all the right people, and belonged to all the right clubs. But after his conversion he said, "Whatever was to my profit I now consider loss for the sake of Christ. What is more, I consider everything a loss compared to the surpassing greatness of knowing Christ Jesus my Lord, for whose sake I have lost all things" (Philippians 3:7,8).

Like Christ—who gave up everything and, becoming a servant, bowed his heart down and died for you and me—Paul had to give up all the other things he had counted on and gained confidence from. He had to lay his human credentials to rest. In a sense, he had to die.

And then, to a group of churches in Galatia, Paul gave this insight: "I have been crucified with Christ and I no longer live, but Christ lives in me. The life I live in the body, I live by faith in the Son of God, who loved me and gave himself for me" (Galatians 2:20).

As one Christian martyr said, "He is no fool who gives up what he cannot keep, to gain what he cannot lose." Paul had given up what he could not keep. He had gained what he could not lose . . . a new life. The life that raised Christ from the dead was now in Paul. Paul was experiencing a supernatural aliveness he had never known before—even in the midst of pain and turmoil and dismay.

But first he had to die. Only then could Paul live a new life. Jesus taught this simple truth very clearly. The key to being the greatest was to be the least. Jesus said, "If anyone would come after me, he must deny himself and take up his cross and follow me. For whoever wants to save his life will lose it, but whoever loses his life for me and for the gospel will save it" (Mark 8:34,35).

God delights in blessing His bondservants with new life, a different spirit, an ability to find life and fullness in the midst of pain, and the courage to face life's agonies. I thank God that He has given me a measure of the courage that Kyle had in his life and death. God has given me a new life, a life that far outweighs the weight of death and loss.

At first I was sure I had gone through enough dying for one lifetime. But as the Spirit of God worked in my life, I realized that I actually had less to give up at this point than at any other in my life. I had tried everything else, and it had not worked. You too may find yourself in this position. This may well be the best time in your life to let go of everything else. He is there waiting to lift you above your pain.

Finishing the Course

> Perseverance must finish its work so that you may be mature and complete, not lacking anything (James 1:4).

Phyllis came to visit me after her husband of many years died suddenly in a tragic accident. At that time her life was turned upside down.

Over a period of several months I was amazed and refreshed to see Phyllis work through her tangled web of emotions. I rejoiced to see this special woman turn her focus from her pain to her heavenly Father and His promise of life in the midst of pain.

Then, after about three months, she missed an appointment. Then another. Finally, I received a brief note: "I have met a man who has the time and money to lift me out of this pit of despair. Thank you for your help. We were married last week."

Was there anything wrong with Phyllis getting married? No, not at all, except if she used marriage to short-cut the process that God wanted to work in her heart—the process of learning perseverance.

One of the most tragic mistakes I see people in pain making is beginning to grow and then bailing out and going backward. They quit instead of finishing the course, not realizing that in doing so that the pain will remain, and the joy will not stay.

God promises that He will not allow us to go through more pain than we can handle. He will supply us with everything we need to go through that painful time successfully (1 Corinthians 10:13). He knows our limits. He even knows how much we can stretch in our faith to trust Him and grow in endurance.

Do not cut the process short. Hang in there. Trust God to get you through—even if you can't see the other side of your grief.

Over the years I have enjoyed watching and playing tennis. I have learned that tennis is every bit as much a game of the mind as it is of the body. Each player is trying to get an edge on the other. It is amazing to see the shifts of momentum.

Sometimes I will be playing someone who appears absolutely flawless. My only hope is that he makes enough mistakes to spare me complete humiliation. Part of me says there is no way I can win two out of three sets. But another part of me has learned to hang in there and keep at it—it's not over until the winning point is scored. And amazingly, things often turn around. My opponent will lose his edge; and if I have kept going, I will be ready to take advantage of the opportunity. I've learned the wisdom of not quitting in tennis.

The same is true of pain. There are times when it seems insurmountable. There is a part of me that wants to throw in the towel. But there is another part of me that doesn't want to cut the process of growth short. I want to know what lies beyond.

That is what James says. "Perseverance must finish its work so that you may be mature and complete." We all want to be more mature. We all want to be more completely who God designed us to be. We're not sure we can make it. But we can. We have God's word on it.

I've learned to stop fighting and resisting my heavenly Father. The pain is not evil and bad. It just hurts. There are worse things than hurting, like not growing. I've learned the wisdom of hanging in there and enduring the pain, the fulfillment and satisfaction in climbing above a mountain of difficulty. I've also learned the joy of maturing in my relationship with my strong and loving Father. The joy is there even when the pain remains. The joy helps me through the pain.

The Place of Prayer

When Kyle died, I prayed a great deal. But most of my prayers were venting my emotions and telling God how much I hurt. I spent little time asking God to help me know how to make life work the way it should in the midst of my pain.

And when I did begin to ask God for something, it was the wrong thing. I would ask God to take away my pain or to somehow bring Kyle back to us. Both requests were out of touch with real life.

Slowly I learned to pray that God would help me experience His joy in the midst of my pain. I began to pray that our family could trust God more. I asked for the courage to endure the pain and not quit. I asked God to help us keep growing and maturing in our relationship with Him and with each other.

Prayer isn't just the movement of our lips; it's the bowing of our hearts before our Lord and Master—our God and Father. It is the pride in our lives getting down on its knees before Almighty God. God isn't interested in lip-service. He wants our hearts, our pride, our very lives.

James tells us how to pray this way. "If any of you lacks wisdom, he should ask God, who gives generously to all without finding fault, and it will be given to him" (James 1:5).

Wisdom is knowing how to make life work the way it should. And the key to getting this wisdom is to ask God. Later James warns us that we do not have because we do not ask. When we ask for wisdom, God will respond. He will give to us generously, not holding anything back. That is just like our Father—wanting to bless us more than we can imagine.

Instead of fighting the agony of your loss, ask for God's joy and confidence and perseverance and completeness in your relationship with Him. He's your Father. He knows what you need, and He wants to help you learn to live again. You need only ask. And then hang in there long enough to see Him come through for you.

CHAPTER 14

Loving Again

*The alternative to loving again is losing
even more.*

FOR THE PEOPLE LEFT by death's shattering visitation, the journey through grief can be a chilling and lonely experience. The person left by death is forced to start over. But they do not want to begin life anew. They cannot live as if their loved one was never there. Often they are left cold, broken, and all alone. The separation between two loved ones is an unending gulf.

For the one who dies, death is a once-and-for-all event. But for the ones left by death, learning to live with the loss of a loved one is a process. It is a process the person does not want to go through. It is painful, unwanted, and seemingly never-ending. It can stretch and deepen us, but to some extent the sense of loss and loneliness never go away.

The person who believes confidently in life after death, and whose loved one shared that confidence, can cling to the powerful hope that they will see each other again. This promise of a happy future may give them the strength to keep going, but hope for the future does not eliminate pain in the present. The day-to-day reality faced by the widow is that she will never again be held by her husband in this life. They will never again hold hands as they take strolls under autumn skies. They will never again joke and laugh or hurt and cry together. They will never again watch the sunset together. They will never again lie beside each other in bed and talk together and love together.

Life will never be the same again. One of the people who had made life's journey more joyous by their presence is now gone. I don't remember when, but I finally spoke the words above my sobbing heart, "Kyle is dead. He is gone. I will never see my precious son grow up. I will never throw the football with him again. I will never again help him learn how to grip a bat or clap for joy because he hit a ball. I will never again sit by his side and read to him at bedtime. I will never again go for walks with him and hear him growing up as he talks with me. I will never see the man he would have become."

Though I have said these things often in the years since his death, the death of my son is still somewhat unreal to me. I can still imagine what Kyle would be like as a teenager. I wonder what college he would have chosen to attend. I can picture the kind of student he would be, and the kinds of professions he would be interested in. I find myself still being a dad to Kyle... only without him here with me. I wish I could say otherwise. I simply cannot.

He is gone. Death has taken him, but my heart still holds him tight, wishing with all my might that I could bring him back. I am sure, by now, that it will always be so. I will never totally believe he is gone and that his life is no longer here with us. Sometimes I get busy with work or activities, but as soon as the busyness subsides, the hurt and the desire to hold my son creep back in and take up residence all over again.

Death viciously stole Kyle from our home. Death emptied my arms. Death is a thief! I could not stop it from stealing my son's life or the life of anyone else in my family. However, if I have learned anything in these years, it is this: Death cannot steal my joy of living or my ability to love again. If these are gone, it is because I have given them up. Death may relentlessly and ruthlessly steal away life, but it can never take away my choice of how to respond. I must choose that personally.

To have loved and lost can often make us wary of ever loving again. It is painful to have given your heart to someone only to have it thrown back at you by death. The expectant couple who loses their child at six months, the husband who loses his wife, the sister who loses her brother—every loss we face takes a part of our heart and a portion of our love with it.

But the alternative to loving again is losing even more. Sometimes in protecting ourselves from more lost love, we forget that the joy of true love is in the loving, not in the return on the investment. Each of us who have experienced the loss of a loved one needs to choose to love again, more and more, as we are able. Love will not make the loss go away, but it helps make life worth living in spite of the loss. These words from C.S. Lewis were a spark that helped Judy and me continue to give our love in spite of the risk:

> To love at all is to be vulnerable. Love anything, and your heart will certainly be wrung and possibly broken. If you want to make sure of keeping it intact, you must give your heart to no one, not even to an animal. Wrap it carefully round with hobbies and little luxuries; avoid all entanglements; lock it up safe in the casket or coffin of your selfishness. But in that casket—safe, dark, motionless, airless—it will change. It will not be broken; it will become unbreakable.[1]

My father's arms still agonize the loss of my son. But somehow, in the midst of my pain and conflicting emotions, God has made a way for me to live on, with aching arms, but a full heart, a heart full of love. I must choose to let God keep doing that. I have found that I must be open and available to my heavenly Father's comfort and care. He provides it lavishly. I must be willing to accept what He gives.

There have been times when I wondered if I would make it. Usually those were the times that I was resisting what God was wanting to do in my life through my loss. Times when I was either focusing on my pain, or angry with God for letting all this happen. But God's promise to be with us and to comfort us in all of our sorrows has remained steadfast. He is always there. He is always good. He is always tender in our time of pain.

During those hard times God's arms will often wrap around Judy and me through a loving note from a friend or a precious memory of the joy we shared. Sometimes God's peace that passes all my understanding will come over us unexpectedly at a particularly desperate time.

God has not been a casual observer in Kyle's death or in my struggle. Nor is He in yours. From where you are the road ahead may seem impossible. But as you face each day—both the good days and the hard, bitter days—He will be there, available to help you as you learn to love again.

CHAPTER 15

The God of
All Comfort

Though he brings grief,
he will show compassion,
so great is his unfailing love.
For he does not willingly bring affliction
or grief to the children of men.

♦ Lamentations 3:32,33

IT IS UNCANNY how God used so many people, some of whom we have never met, to comfort us in our time of need. Cards, letters, phone calls, visits—all came our way. We needed them. God used these blessed people to bring us compassion and comfort. But very soon God was putting us in their shoes.

A few weeks after Kyle's death we were back in that same hospital waiting for our daughter, Kelly, to be born. Labor and delivery were difficult and, understandably, very emotional for Judy. To have buried one child and now be giving birth to another in a matter of weeks would weigh on any mother's heart. I felt so helpless. I knew there were little things I could do, but she had to work so many things out in her own head and heart.

After Kelly's birth, Judy was in recovery for a few days. She was in a semiprivate room with a young woman who had delivered premature twins. The twins were very small and life was difficult, but they were struggling with everything they had to survive. The doctors were very cautious—there was the very real possibility that one or both would die in minutes, days, or weeks.

This new mother of two was agonizing for her children, hoping they would not die, but knowing they surely could. Then she found out Judy had lost a son just weeks before. She felt that same bond of attraction and need for Judy that Judy and I had felt when our physician friend had shared his heartache and pain with us.

Judy did not feel like helping someone else. But there she was. And there was a strange tugging within Judy to do what was best, even though it was painful. God had used Dr. Knarr to bring Judy and me comfort in our time of need. He had used him to minister to us. In the process we had ministered to him. Now God was using Judy to help her roommate. And He used the process to help Judy.

Just four months later one of the twin boys died in the night. The mom asked Judy to come and be with her at the funeral. Judy wept at the thought of burying another young boy. But she went. That was God's design to bring comfort and ministry into our lives, and into the lives of others through us.

There were soon people in my life as well who were strengthened by what we were going through. Gerald was in his early sixties and newly retired when he lost his wonderful wife after a 28-year bout with cancer. They had lovingly cared for their marriage, and their beautifully intertwined lives accentuated his sense of loss when she was finally torn away from him. Gerald and I met for many months, and he gained comfort not only from my concern as a pastor, but from my experience as a companion who had also lost someone near.

Within a year or so Judy and I were being asked to speak in Death and Dying classes at the university. Each time we felt God's arms of compassion and tender comfort all over again. That helped us. But so did the help we could give others.

So now, years later, here I sit, writing a book, crying half the time, but being so blessed by my Father.

The apostle Paul wrote about the Father's promised comfort and ministry out of his own need. In fact, he wrote these words to the Corinthians:

> We do not want you to be uninformed, brothers, about the hardships we suffered in the province of Asia. We were under great pressure, far beyond our ability to endure, so that we despaired even of life. Indeed, in our hearts we felt the sentence of death. But this happened that we might not rely on ourselves but on God, who raises the dead (2 Corinthians 1:8,9).

Paul says that he felt the sentence of death. Yet even in his despair he says that all this happened so that "we may not rely on ourselves but on God." Total reliance on the Father is what must happen for us if we are to embrace God's compassion and comfort and willingly embrace the difficult task of helping others. Someone just like you needs to feel the arms of God through your arms; to hear God's tender, understanding voice through your voice. Let God enfold you, and you will be able to enfold others. Look. Listen. And then let Him use you to help someone else. The comfort and joy you experience will surprise you.

Help from the Spirit

Along with the help that comes from learning to help others, God also promises to encourage us and comfort us through His Spirit. During a time when the church in Rome was suffering, Paul revealed these two promises:

> In the same way, the Spirit helps us in our weakness. We do not know what we ought to pray for, but the Spirit himself intercedes for

us with groans that words cannot express. And he who searches our hearts knows the mind of the Spirit, because the Spirit intercedes for the saints in accordance with God's will.

And we know that in all things God works for the good of those who love him, who have been called according to his purpose (Romans 8:26-28).

God cares so very much for you and me. He hurts with our hurt. He feels with us in our aloneness, dismay, guilt, and fear. He agonizes over our deep sense of loss and frustration.

He has given us the Holy Spirit to help us in our weakness. We may not know what to pray about, but the Holy Spirit does. And the Spirit prays for us with groanings too deep for words.

In His groaning the Spirit does something that will help us. He intercedes for us. He steps into the presence of Almighty God and asks for the very things we need to rise above the pain of loss. His are perfect prayers. They will be answered. The Father will respond and lift us up in our time of need.

Not only that, but the Father promises that He will cause all things to work together for good. He is not promising to make our loss "good." But He does make it clear that He will arrange and order and design things so that "good" will come out of our painful, frustrating loss in life. He can bring good out of anything: our right-on-the-target decisions and those that are completely off the wall. Those situations we understand, and those we do not have a clue about. Right prayers and selfish prayers.

After all these years, I still want Kyle back. I would give up anything that was mine to give if it would restore him to us. The loss of a loved one is a permanent condition in this lifetime, but God promises to change other things so that we can rise above the pain and live a full life above the "missing" and the agony of loss.

Though I would give anything of mine to have Kyle back, I know that is not a part of God's plan for this life. He loves Kyle too much to bring him back. And He has other things in mind for me—good things that I would not have any other way. I am thankful to have grown, thankful to be the "me" that I am now and not the "me" I was before.

The Spirit of God, who lives within me, has prayed for me with a heart of compassion and concern. He has prayed for me in ways I did not even realize were important. And my Father has responded by changing things to work for my good. He has changed *me* . . . forever.

CHAPTER 16

A Glorious
Future

*He will wipe every tear from their eyes. There will be no
more death or mourning or crying or pain....*

✦ Revelation 21:4

THE DAY IS COMING when death will ultimately be destroyed. Paul teaches this clearly in 1 Corinthians 15:20-26:

> But Christ has indeed been raised from the dead, the firstfruits of those who have fallen asleep. For since death came through a man, the resurrection of the dead comes also through a man. For as in Adam all die, so in Christ all will be made alive.... Then the end will come, when he hands over the kingdom to God the Father after he has destroyed all dominion, authority and power. For he must reign until he has put all his enemies under his feet. The last enemy to be destroyed is death.

Death entered this world through the man, Adam. And through another man the resurrection from death has been introduced into the formula of life and eternity. When Jesus was raised from the dead, not only did He receive freedom from death, but His resurrection foreshadowed the time when we all will be raised from the dead. Those who belong to Him will spend eternity with their Lord—and death will be destroyed.

Not only will we be freed from the jaws of death, we will be given a new kind of life. We will be changed even more—forever. Paul makes this clear:

> So will it be with the resurrection of the dead. The body that is sown is perishable, it is raised imperishable; it is sown in dishonor, it is raised in glory; it is sown in weakness, it is raised in power; it is sown a natural body, it is raised a spiritual body. If there is a natural body, there is also a spiritual body. So it is written: "The first man Adam became a living being; the last Adam, a life-giving spirit" (1 Corinthians 15:42-45).

When we die, we are perishable, dishonorable, weak, and fleshly. But when we are raised, we will be imperishable, with glory and power, and we will be fully alive spiritually. We were born in the likeness of sinful and fallen Adam. But God will lift up His own and "so shall we bear the likeness of the man from heaven," our Master, Jesus Christ (1 Corinthians 15:49).

A day is coming when our Father will raise Kyle and me and our whole family along with all believers. We will be with Him forever. And we will be changed in many ways—thank God! I look forward to that great reunion day when my Father lifts us up to a better life, forever, with Him.

Having said this, I am aware that some will rightfully ask, "But what if I or a loved one I've lost does not belong to God? Or we are not sure?"

In Luke 16, Jesus tells the story of a rich man who despised God during his life, and then was separated from Him in his death. The rich man was in torment. As he looked on the earth, he felt compassion for his brothers and asked if God could send someone to warn them so they would not make the same mistake as he. It grieved him to see his brothers heading for this place of torment as well. But the Father denied his request, telling him that if the brothers did not respond to what God had already sent them, neither would they respond to someone rising from the dead and telling them (Luke 16:19-31).

To be honest, none of us knows "absolutely" who belongs to the Father and who does not. John tells us that we can know for ourselves, but nothing is given us to know for sure about another. But based on this story by Jesus and verses in Hebrews 11:40–12:3 which also indicate that those in the faith who have gone on before us are in some sense witnesses of us, no matter where a lost one is at, with the Father or separated from Him, they are very much aware of you and the life you are living. They care about you and want the best for you, just as the rich man in Jesus' story cared about his brothers and wanted the best for them. And it grieves them if you are not willing to accept God on His terms during this life, just as it did the rich man for his brothers.

Could I encourage you, if you are not in a right relationship with your Father, that you make the decision to get down on your knees and humble yourself before Him? Seek, and you will find. Ask, and it will be given to you. Knock, and the door will be opened. Like the prodigal son, your Father is waiting for your return home. Listen to these words of hope from Paul:

> Listen, I tell you a mystery: We will not all sleep, but we will all be changed—in a flash, in the twinkling of an eye, at the last trumpet. For the trumpet will sound, the dead will be raised imperishable, and we will be changed. For the perishable must clothe itself with the imperishable, and the mortal with immortality. When the perishable has been clothed with the imperishable, and the mortal with immortality, then the saying that is written will come true:

"Death has been swallowed up in victory.
Where, O death, is your victory? Where, O
death, is your sting?" (1 Corinthians 15:51-55).

Every believer will be changed . . . forever! Death will
be swallowed up in victory. Death is a defeated foe. The
resurrection has taken the ultimate sting out of death.
Death is not a final condition. What a promise to claim!

Our Father has indeed promised us a new life in the
future, but the Bible is quite emphatic that His fullness of
life is available to us right now, even when we are facing
the loss of a loved one.

CHAPTER 17

The Promise
of Life

God loves life; he invented it.

✦ Paul Tournier

I USED TO look to "normalcy" as the equilibrium in my life, the thing that kept life stable and seemingly safe. Kyle's death has helped me to set aside this fantasy and instead look to the Lord Himself, the Lord of life and love and hope and promise. I live now absolutely convinced that the Lord Himself is the only stability in life. And how secure He is; how secure and confident He makes me feel.

Missing Kyle has lost its edge over the years in direct proportion to my focus on and trust in the Lord who is my shepherd. There are occasions when Judy and I are still overcome with a sense of loss. But that is okay. I am not afraid of sorrow or pain anymore. By God's grace I have found His fullness of real life to far outweigh any pain or suffering I might have to face. My Father has been gracious in the midst of my sorrow, patient with my anger, loving in my sense of loss, and dependable in lifting me up above my heartache as I bow the knees of my heart before Him.

I live my life now in view of and not in avoidance of death. I plan for the future, but I live for today. My priorities have changed. "Getting ahead" is getting farther behind on my list of things to do. The little things that I used to worry about seem so petty today. I have realized that pride and self-centeredness are death's first cousins. They rob us of the abilities to give and love and forgive. They make life empty and shallow. They steal the joys of loving today with their promises of pleasure tomorrow, making us two-time losers: We waste today, and tomorrow never comes.

My confidence in and respect for God has grown. That too has helped to alter and broaden my perspective on life. There is more to my life than what happens in my lifetime on earth. Life is more than existence; it has a purpose. God infuses it with meaning. I live for Him and not myself, and I trust Him more than I can ever trust myself. I want to honor Him for who He is and thank Him for all He gives and promises, including the promise of life forever with Him.

Kyle used to love to draw and paint and color. One evening when our family was walking along, one of the boys looked at the sunset and pointing, exclaimed, "Hey, Mom and Dad. Look! I bet God's letting Kyle paint the sunset! He's doing such a good job!"

Kyle may not be painting the sunsets, but we believe that he is enjoying them, and someday we will enjoy them with him and the rest of God's family. Our lives will once again be totally changed—forever.

If you ask me how things are with me now, I will tell you:

> Death is a big deal; I take it very seriously.
> God has my attention; I take my relationship with Him very seriously.

> Death is not a friend; it is an enemy. I hate it passionately.
> God has proved to be more than a friend. I love Him deeply.

> Death has taught me how to cry.
> My Father has engulfed me with His tender arms of compassion.

Death will come my way again.
My Father will see me through.

Death made me want to die with my son.
God has given me life beyond my wildest dreams.

Death tried to change my mind about God.
God has changed my life forever. I am blessed.

Is There Really a Loving God?

Why are you downcast, O my soul?
Why so disturbed within me?
Put your hope in God....

✦ Psalm 42:5

GOD HAS MADE US a fabulous offer: to live above the difficulties of life. Not without pain, but above its demeaning, devastating blow. He has promised that we can experience real life—above our expectations—even if our lives have been changed forever by the death of someone near.

Maybe you are wrestling with God. Perhaps you question why, if there is a God, did He allow someone close to you to die? Is the idea of a loving, personal God just so much wishful thinking?

If this is how you feel right now, this chapter is designed especially for you. As you read, you will discover that many of our thoughts and feelings, and nature itself, point to a God who is worthy of our trust, even when bad things happen.

Our Denials Point to God

"God! Why did you take him?"

Why is it so common to blame God when death comes close to us? Some people declare that since a good God would never allow such suffering and misery and death in the world, God must not exist.

But if there is no God, then why do we lash out at Him—emotionally, intellectually? Do we not innately admit the possibility of God by blaming or denying Him because of death? Somehow, almost all of us associate God with death. The two seem to go hand in hand. Why is that? Could it be that we inwardly acknowledge the existence of God when we are faced with death, but emotionally we deny that sense of reality that we feel within?

The very act of blaming or denying God for death implies we sense, or in some way admit, the possibility of His existence. Our denials and blamings point to the possibility of the existence of God, and therefore to *hope* for life after death. Our moral outrage leads us in the same direction. When we feel and reason that death is morally wrong, unjust, and unfair, we assume standards of good and bad that are beyond our existence. If we are nothing but animals, and there is no higher moral law, then we should never feel resentment or disgust over the seeming injustices of life and death. But we do feel these things.

"Goodness" is a moral quality. Animals are not moral beings; humans are. Therefore, humans have a different nature than animals . . . a seemingly higher nature . . . a *moral* nature. If we are not higher than animals in this sense, where did we get our moral standards and why do we resist the possibility of yet another and higher form of being and life?

If there were no God, the only sensible thing for us to do would be to become pure pragmatists, doing only what logic dictated. The logical course of action would be to strive for our own individual welfare, caring little or nothing about other people. In such a scenario, nothing would be "wrong"; certain things would simply be less useful to our advancement than others.

Wait a minute! Does that sound familiar? Like our world today? Something inside each of us struggles with the idea of living in a godless, completely pragmatic world. So what lures us to that kind of life if not our self-centered human natures? And how are we able to resist except through the moral quality in us? So much mental, emotional, and even physical suffering exists in the world today because we choose to live in opposition to our own moral side. Every time we feel the pains of death, and cry out inside that it is unfair, we need to ask ourselves, "Who said it was unfair?" If there is no God, and we are but happenstance products of a different animal species, then death is natural. *But it is not natural. It is not good.* We know that. Without the existence of God, moral justice would be little more than a philosophical term that has no bearing on life at all. Our only law would be that every man should do what is right in his own eyes.

But it seems that there are moral laws in the world; moral laws not made by man, but agreed upon by man; moral laws that transcend man, and which man senses. However, as with any law, these transcendent moral laws can be broken. And when they are broken, the consequences that follow become devastating. Nations, societies, and entire civilizations have fallen because they persisted in living life contrary to inwardly known, but outwardly violated, transcendent moral laws.

This, it seems, is consistent with the Christian proclamation. The apostle Paul wrote:

> Now the holy anger of God is disclosed from Heaven against the godlessness and evil of those men who render the truth dumb and impotent by their wickedness. It is not that they do not know the truth about God; indeed, he has made it quite plain to [literally "within"] them. For since the beginning of the world the invisible attributes of God, for example, his eternal power and divinity, have been plainly

discernible through things which he has made and which are commonly seen and known, thus leaving these men without a rag of excuse. They knew all the time that there is a God, yet they refuse to acknowledge him as such, or to thank him for what he is or does (Romans 1:18-21 Phillips).

God has made Himself known "within" every person, and He holds them accountable to recognize and respond to Him. Yet, Paul says, there are many who do not respond, and they suffer the consequences. That same passage continues to explain that the consequences come as God allows them to live their contrary way of life to its ultimate conclusion. God does not want this, but neither will He force people to listen to Him. He respects them and their choices, even when they choose self-destructive ways of life. By allowing people to stumble along on their chosen path, God hopes that they will turn back and recognize Him and call upon Him to help them live life as He intended it.

Frankly, there are many people today who are looking for excuses not to accept what they sense inside themselves is true—the reality of God. And we are beginning to live with, and dread, many of the horrors that come when every person does what is right in his own eyes. We deplore what is going on around us. We despise what is going on within ourselves. Yet we close our eyes and hope it will get better soon. Maybe the next president will make it go away. Maybe this school or that speaker will make everything better. And yet the world keeps heading downhill, and we continue to be alarmed by death.

Why are we so reluctant to ask what we know is the real question: "What is the true source of the downhill trends today?" We want to blame the problem on legislators or somebody else, but inside we know that it is our own choices, and those of others, which are taking us in the direction we are going.

All of this simply reinforces the feasibility of the existence of the God of the Bible and the hope that He will provide us with life after death. All our denials and inner struggles can only lead to one logical conclusion when all the facts are considered: Our wrestlings, our denials, our blamings, our cursing of death, all point to the very real possibility of a higher order of moral being, of a God who offers hope for life beyond death—life that is significantly more fulfilling and meaningful than life as we know it now.

Nature Points to God

Besides what the Bible says about God and the promise of life after death, other signs point to God as well. Nature, all around us, is one of them.

We all know that unless a seed falls to the ground and dies, it cannot bear new life. Seeds have to die if they are to experience regeneration. Why should we not assume at least the strong possibility that the same type of event might occur for human beings as well?

The seasons give us multitudes of illustrations of this process. We see trees lose their leaves and become bare and seemingly lifeless for months at a time, only to be struck with wonder when spring comes and new life bursts forth. In fact, the trees seem to be more alive than they were before they shed all their leaves in the fall. "Dying" precedes "living" throughout nature. Is not the same reality at least a possible consideration for men and women, boys and girls?

But nature offers us more hope. The world around us teaches us that there are different and distinct levels of nature. We hear talk about our *human* nature all the time. But other forms of life have a nature as well. Each living thing on earth has a nature unique to its kind. Flowers have a different nature than animals. Animals have different natures than humans. Man has yet another, higher nature. Do the principles of causation not point to a Creator with an even higher nature than man? Why do we resist this?

Is it because nature gives us no clues? No, nature supports such a real possibility. Nature displays stages of natures that lead to man and beyond. Nature truly does offer us hope that there can be life after death. We are also given reason from nature for a real hope that there can be a personal being in existence with a higher nature than our own. Nature gives no guarantees, but it supplies ample support for such a possibility—a possibility that we need to take seriously. If the God of the Bible is just such a being, as I believe He is, then we can have the confidence that He will give us a new and more vital life with Him after death and forever.

Our Fantasies Point to God

Whether we believe that there is a loving God just beyond death's door or not, we all have to live with the reality of death around us. As one author reminds us: "Nothing is more certain in life than the fact of death. It is confirmed to us every day we live. We read about it in every daily newspaper. There is death by disease, accident, murder, starvation, drowning. No city newspaper has ever had cause to omit the obituary column!"[1] Death is all around us. We too will face death someday, but we would just as soon not think about it. To be honest, we would like to wish it away. And we try—more than we may be willing to admit.

We all have subtle ways of closing off unpleasantness from our lives. Many of us live with death by denying it. Many of us live with death by keeping busy and trying to ignore it. These are common. But in our day and time, in our culture of luxury and comfort, there is an ever-increasing way we try to live with death—through fantasy.

When our family lived in Florida, our favorite place to visit was Disneyworld. It was proclaimed a "wonderland." And it was. It is. It is a magical place where fun and excitement and enchantment are etched on every pillar and face. It is spotless. Everything is in its place. Every attendant smiles. All the stories have happy endings. Even the mechanical animals that die resurrect to sing and shout again. There is no death in Disneyworld! Children love a fantasyland. But so do adults. All of us would like life to be perfect, spotless, fun, and deathless. We would love to see life as smiles, rosy cheeks, and thrills one after another with no thought of death.

Our society has become more and more perfectionistic. We get mad if the house is not spotless when we come home. We fuss at the child who is not doing "the best" on school assignments. We fret if we do not make more and more money so we can buy more and more things. We strive for the job with a few more fringe benefits and increasing comfort and prestige. We want power: pure, perfect power. Then, we tell ourselves, life will be like it should be, now and forever.

But then something unexpected happens. You are diagnosed with cancer. Or a loved one dies in an accident. Your world of make-believe begins to cave in all around you, and you are buried under an unfathomable heap of "reality." Life and death have barged into your sheltered and fanciful space and cruelly wrenched away your hopes.

Fantasies of hope have always been with us. The ancients wrote fanciful stories of superhuman heroes who were beyond death and who could save helpless mortals. Many ancient Greek children fantasized that Mercury would wing down and spare them. Today we have Superman and a hoard of others that dominate the imaginations of most children. We are raising a generation of children who would rather watch "Super-Heroes" on television than play a game or go for a hike. Our fantasy carries on.

Even the arts in our world have traditionally dealt with death with gentle sceneries and calming tones. Where is the dirge of death admitted? Where are the horrors depicted? That is radical! That is improper. Only in our minds is death gentle and calm.

If there is no God of love as described in the Bible, then what is our hope? There is no *real* hope; only fantasized hope. Only make-believe and denial and the closing of the eyes. If the God of love is there, then we can have real hope. Not a hope that we will be spared the agony of physical death, but confidence that death is not the victor. It wins the battle; we win the war. It brings temporary separation; God brings back wholeness and eternal life. Death will still need to be reckoned with, but its sting is gone.

One of the greatest dangers in believing in the God of hope is that we may believe in Him as we believe in a fantasy. There are so many who believe in God and trust in Him the same way a child believes and trusts in Superman. If we believe in God because we have outgrown Superman, then we too are imaging a fantasy God.

But if we believe in the God of Christianity, the God of the Bible, then we need to be convinced of His existence based upon objective evidence, not wishful thinking. Our wishes do not make God real. God is real because He is real, not because we hope He is. If the God of the Bible is real, then He calls the shots; we don't. He gives the options; not us.

The God of the Bible makes it perfectly clear that we must accept His Son, Jesus, for who He claimed to be and what He claimed to do. The Bible says even the demons believe God exists and tremble before Him. The

God of the Bible makes it clear that faith in Jesus is the only way to heaven. Considering the stakes involved and the fickleness of death's timing, it only seems wise to investigate the claims of Jesus. The decision you make will affect your eternal destiny as well as your life and ability to face death with confidence.

Final Words to the Jury

When we contemplate our own death or the death of a friend or loved one, we experience a vast gulf. That deep sense of separation makes us question if there really is a God. How could a loving God allow such misery in the first place?

As I examined other religions and philosophies and the alternatives they offer to such a difficult question, I became convinced Christianity was by far the most concerned with presenting its perspective on death, and the most able to present credible evidence of its faith (see Appendix B). As I evaluated Christianity's case for God, I found that the testimonies seemed clear and consistent. And the witnesses seemed as credible as any witnesses could possibly be. I was not convinced of the case for Christianity with 100 percent proof, but I was convinced "beyond a reasonable doubt."

I continue to have questions and doubts about the nature and existence of God. Questions and doubts are part of our humanness, but they seldom, if ever, prove or settle anything. If I doubt that God exists, especially as I feel the pain of death, it is my doubt that needs to be investigated further. If God exists, He exists whether I doubt it or question it or believe it. Doubts are open doors that need to be investigated more thoroughly.

I believe that God is real, not because I have been told to believe it, and not because I want it to be true, but because of the overwhelmingly convincing evidence presented by Jesus, the Bible, science, humankind, and even nature and philosophy. Believing in God has changed my perspective. It has given me hope. But it did not answer all my questions about life after death. If there is a God, as described in the Bible, then life after death is real. But what kind of life might it be?

The Gospel of John records these words of Jesus: "I am the way and the truth and the life. No one comes to the Father except through me" (John 14:6). Jesus is claiming to be the path, or means, to true life, which is found in the presence of His Father. These words challenged me to keep searching. In Matthew's Gospel, Jesus says, "Ask and it will be given to you; seek and you will find; knock and the door will be opened to you. For anyone who asks receives; he who seeks finds; and to him who knocks, the door will be opened" (Matthew 7:7,8). I took this as a promise from a supernatural God that if I would keep searching for the path to true life, He would make sure I found it.

Another passage from the Bible made the subject even clearer. Speaking of Jesus, the apostle John wrote: "He was in the world, and the world was made through Him, and the world did not know Him. He came to His own, and those who were His own did not receive Him. But as many as received Him, to them He gave the right to become children of God, even to those who believe in His name" (John 1:10-12 NASB).

John was revealing to us that Jesus is the Creator of the universe and all living creatures including humanity. But His created beings did not recognize Him, so He came to live among them. For the most part, His creation refused to accept Him for who He was. But all who did accept Him for who He claimed to be were given the right to be children of God and to live eternally with God. The key was putting their trust in Him.

As John writes this gospel account, he makes it clear that each individual needs to decide if he or she believes that Jesus was who He claimed to be (God) and that He accomplished what He claimed to accomplish (providing the way to live with God forever).

The Bible gives a rationale for this. According to the Bible, God created the world out of nothing and designed a man and a woman to live here on the earth. God patterned them after Himself and created an environment that was conducive to and compatible with their design. However, one inherent feature of God in humankind was the ability to *choose*. Both the man and the woman chose to live life contrary to God's design and stated pattern for them. Because of this rebellion to God's design, they could no longer enjoy all the benefits of God's creation, and, worst of all, they experienced a deep separation from their Creator. They had chosen a contrary way of life, which, by its very nature, created a chasm between them and God.

All mankind has chosen that same contrary way of life. We too experience that deep rift with God, not by His choice, but by our own.

But God loved His creation and wanted to spare it from a perpetual life of separation from Himself and a miserable life lived contrary to His intended design. God wanted to restore our torn relationship so we could enjoy Him and the life He intended. Death, both relationally and physically, was the result of each person's choice to live life contrary to God's design.

God allowed physical death to continue. Otherwise the spiral of pain and misery brought on by trying to live differently than we were designed to live would never end. In a small way we resemble a machine that has slipped a gear. We have to turn off the power (through physical death) before we can hope to fix it. But the aim in stopping it is to help it function smoothly again. So God allowed physical death to continue. He had to because He is a just God. But because He is also a loving God, He made it possible to restore our relationship with

Him—thereby allowing us to live and enjoy life as it was intended.

The way that God did this was very costly to Himself. He sent his Son, Jesus, to live among us as the perfect God, dwelling in a physical body just like yours and mine, with all its frailties. He lived a perfect life, the kind of life God intended for us to be able to live. Therefore, Jesus, the only perfect person to ever live, did not have to experience the physical death that results from aborting God's design for living. Nonetheless he died. Not because He needed to for Himself, but because He wanted to for us—to restore our relationship with our God; to close that gulf of separation. He took all of *our* sins on Himself and died to end the spiritual separation between God and man, so that we could have a fulfilling life forever with Him after our physical death. But He still leaves the choice to accept the gift of eternal life to us.

If God had given us life forever as we know it now, we would be pitiful creatures indeed. He allows physical death to continue, but He has provided a vital hope for what lies behind death's door. God and His home wait for everyone who chooses to accept Jesus as God's Son and our Savior. The price Jesus paid to redeem mankind was physical death on a cross and relational separation from His Father for three days. After three days, as history records, Jesus rose from the dead as God to demonstrate to all who wanted to know that He was Who He claimed and therefore could be trusted to accomplish what He claimed, providing the means to live with God in His home forever.

There is a flow and consistency that makes sense in all that Christianity in the Bible presents. However, I often see a conflict between what Christianity is and claims to be in the Bible, and how those who claim to be Christians live it out today. We have all experienced this. But Christianity never promises that those who accept the claims of Christ will be perfect here and now. It says that those who are truly committed to following Jesus Christ have their eternal destiny settled, and that little by little God is at work in their hearts and lives to transform them into His image. This process will not be finished until this life is over. Less-than-perfect but slowly maturing lives is what Christians should display.

After hearing the case for Christianity, you may still have some doubts. That is to be expected, especially as you may feel the agony of death around you. But weigh the evidence for God's existence "reasonably." If God is there, it makes a significant difference to you. You are staking your life, and your eternity, on it. Your life has been changed. Now God wants to make another change that leads to more life for you—forever.

Empty Religions

*Death is the fundamental human problem, for if death is
final nothing is worthwhile save self-indulgence. And no
philosophy or religion which cannot come to terms with
death is any real use to us.*

✦ James Packer

WHEN STRUGGLING WITH THE LOSS of a loved one, we
long for anything to help us deal with our unwanted
pain. As I looked to my Christian faith and found it
tattered by misconceptions, the beat of the world's voices
kept surfacing into my consciousness, inviting me to
listen and follow. Thankfully I was able to see through
those hopeless fictions.

But there are other ways people try to find help, especially if they have been frustrated by their faith. Other
religions can be appealing in many ways. Often in our
hurting conditions, those of us struggling with a loss are
vulnerable to a "grass-is-greener," "shop-around" attitude regarding faith.

I trust that what follows will help you see very clearly
what these major religions have to offer in the face of
death. You will hear their own words. And I believe you
will see that sincere words are about all they have to
offer. These faiths speak confidently. They give great
promises. But they come up empty.

The Hindu Faith on Death

There is a general consensus among Hindus who accept
reincarnation on the subjects of death and beyond, but

also a general vagueness as to what death really is. Their beliefs about death and reincarnation are best explained from their own philosophical commentaries, called the *Upanishads*, which give account of the secret teachings handed down to those who "sat at the feet" of India's sages dating from the eighth to the sixth century before Christ.[1]

One such *Upanishad* is the *Chandogya*, which is one of the two most ancient Hindu records. It concludes with these words:

> This body is mortal and always held by death. It is the abode of that Self which is immortal and without body. When in the body, by thinking this body is I and I am this body, the Self is held by pleasure and pain. So long as he is in the body, he cannot get free from pleasure and pain. But when he is free of the body, when he knows himself different from the body, then neither pleasure nor pain touches him.[2]

According to these lines, the body is insignificant and not really necessary for a person's true existence. Pain and pleasure are not real, but a part of our improper imagining that the real "I" includes a body. The way to get rid of pain is to come to realize that "I" exists apart from any physical body. Therefore the "I" does not experience pain or pleasure.[3]

In another record, the *Kat'ha Upanishad*, a father is said to have wanted to gain greater progress in this process and so sacrificed his son, Nachiketas. After being his father's child-sacrifice, Nachiketas enters the abode of Yama, the god of death. But no one is there to greet him. Three days later Yama returns home and apologizes for his lack of hospitality. Thereupon he promises to grant young Nachiketas three wishes. After being granted his first two wishes, the young boy requests his third:

Nachiketas: There is that doubt, when a man is dead—some saying, he is; others, he is not. This I should like to know, taught by thee, this is the third of my boons [wishes].

Death [Yama]: On this point even the gods have doubted formerly; it is not easy to understand. That subject is subtle. Choose another boon, O Nachiketas, do not press me, and let me off that boon.[4]

But Nachiketas does press the god of death. Finally, Yama makes this declaration:

Beyond the senses there are the objects, beyond the objects there is the mind, beyond the mind there is the intellect, the Great Self is beyond the intellect. Beyond the Great there is the Undeveloped, beyond the Undeveloped there is the Person (purusha). Beyond the Person there is nothing—this is the goal....

He who has perceived that which is without sound, without touch, without form, without decay, without taste, eternal, without smell, without beginning, without end, beyond the Great, and unchangeable, is freed from the jaws of death.[5]

It is rather odd that the god of death would beg not to have to reveal what happens to a person at death, saying that the gods disagree and the answer is subtle and hard to understand. When Yama gives his final answer, he demonstrates the validity of his hesitation. He essentially concludes that "nothingness" is the ultimate goal of every person. But how can "nothing" be the ultimate "something?" And why would men strive for "nothingness?" Truly this is "subtle and hard to understand."

But if one does desire to attain to nothingness, what is involved? There is no clear answer within Hinduism. Or more precisely, there are so many different and conflicting answers that one is left to choose one and hope he makes the right decision. Some people say the key is mind control, achieved through yoga.[6] Others point to rituals such as observance of study, sacrifice, and almsgiving.[7] Some even go so far as to teach the young, aspiring Hindu to trick other people into sinful acts, thereby giving them his sins and in turn taking on any merit they had. The following is one of many such teachings:

> A man should, without molestation, stand not too far from a crowd of women and not too near, always within their range of sight. Making one young and lovely woman the object of his attentions, he should ogle, solicit, importune, swagger and indulge in similar actions. Though making eyes at a woman is not proper, he should show signs of his passion such as acting as though he was holding the woman by the hair. Then the men, women and eunuchs, who have been talking among themselves, will say, "This fellow is a sex maniac and a womanizer." By that false accusation all their merit will decidedly attach to him, and all his sins to them.[8]

This passage teaches that one can climb the Hindu ladder of success by using other people as stepping-stones, pushing them down so that the aspirant can climb up.

There is much within Hinduism that cannot be covered here. It is a complex and admittedly unclear religion which teaches that a person needs many, many lifetimes to become good enough and acquire enough knowledge to finally achieve the ultimate "nothingness" as part of the universe. It seems odd that after thousands of years and many, many lifetimes, more people are not cleansed from their impurities and imperfect control of their lives to the point that they never experience pain or pleasure and never fear death.

Because of these and many other difficulties, Hinduism has become the mother of many religions, the most famous of which are Jainism, Sikhism, and Buddhism. These all began in an attempt to reform Hinduism. Buddhism has become one of the major world religions.

The Buddhist Faith on Death

In approximately 530 B.C. a wealthy nobleman by the name of Siddhartha Gautama became disenchanted with his Hindu faith. He had submitted himself to several Hindu masters but experienced futility in his quest. This led to his becoming a complete ascetic. After nearly six years of deprivation, Gautama was so weak that he could no longer move or even speak. He was on the verge of death. Fortunately, Gautama was found by a young woman, Sujata, who nursed him back to health.

When Gautama regained his health he is reported to have said, "This have I learned: There is no hope in words alone; no hope in ascetic practices alone. . . . I have been a fool and found a path."[9]

But to what did Gautama believe he had found the path? This can be understood only when we reflect on these parting words of Gautama to his father, a feudal lord:

> If I should delay and death separates me from the quest, then all I have to offer is lost. Perchance my ardor will lead to the conquest of death, and that is worth the effort. Perhaps I can raise the lamp of wisdom before what has

been the darkness of ignorance. Perhaps there is a better way, and I can find it. This is the kingdom I seek, and without pride, without station, without protection, I long to go forth. The world has raised the long banner, and followed the lesser course. The world is troubled, the world is in turmoil, and I myself must live in turmoil until I find release for all who live in the world. This is the kingdom to which I am called.[10]

And then as Gautama turned to take one last look at his home, the palace, he vowed: "Until I conquer old age, disease and death, I shall see you no more!"[11]

Gautama called the path he believed he had discovered—the path to conquering aging, suffering, and dying—the Middle Path. This path avoided the extremes of both asceticism (which nearly killed him) and indulgence (which he grew up with). Instead he practiced meditation. It was during one such time that Gautama claims he became "enlightened" and achieved what is known as *nirvana* while still alive. Thus he became Buddha, meaning the "enlightened one."

One author summarizes Gautama's "path":

The goal of each Buddhist is the attainment of the state of nirvana. Though this word means "to extinguish" or "blow out," it does not imply annihilation but means a release from suffering, desire, and the finite self. Gautama's original teaching was that nirvana is not God or heaven, for his system has no place for death. The Absolute is completely impersonal, and salvation is attained solely by self-effort.[12]

Because this path was based on self-effort, there was quite an extensive list of rules and regulations. Of these rules and the keeping of them, one scholar has noted: "This, however, was far from easy, and Buddha therefore insisted that whoever would enter Nirvana ought first to withdraw from the world and become a monk."[13]

But what did Buddha teach regarding the very subject he set out to conquer? In a short dialogue found in the *Udana*, Buddha says:

> All griefs or lamentations whatso'er
> And diverse forms of sorrow in the world,
> Because of what is dear to these become.
> Things dear not being, these do not become.
> Happy are they therefore and free from grief
> To whom is naught at all dear in the world.
> Wherefore aspiring for the griefless, sorrow-
> less,
> Make thou in all the world naught dear to
> thee.[14]

According to this teaching, Buddha believed that the way to avoid grief, sorrow, pain, and agony is to not let anything become dear to you. If you do not love anyone or anything, it will not hurt to lose it. In one story by the Buddha, a young mother is chided for mourning over the loss of her child. She is told to put away the selfishness of her affection for her dead child. If she did not have affection for her child, she would not mourn its death. If she is ever to achieve nirvana, she must learn to stop loving and caring for others.[15]

But how can a person stop loving or caring about everything? This does not seem realistic or reasonable in the world in which we live. The Buddha gives this reply:

> This assurance is not an assurance of num-
> bers nor logic; it is not the mind that is to be
> assured but the heart. The . . . assurance comes

with the unfolding insight that follows passion—hindrances cleared away, knowledge—
hindrances purified, and egolessness clearly
perceived and patiently accepted. As the mortal-
mind ceases to discriminate [weigh things
out], there is no more thirst for life, no more
sex-lust, no more thirst for learning, no more
thirst for eternal life; with the disappearance
of these fourfold thirsts, there is no more
accumulation of habit-energy; with no more
accumulation of habit-energy the defilements
on the face of the Universal Mind clear away,
and the Bodhisattva attains self-realization of
Noble Wisdom that is the heart's assurance of
Nirvana.[16]

Therefore, the way to achieve the loss of all feelings of
attachment or passion is to stop using one's mind.

Buddhism, as a reform movement of Hinduism, also
believes in reincarnation as the means by which ultimately all human beings will achieve nirvana.[17] In the
end, each person will scale the walls of mere humanity
and achieve Ultimate Nothingness. Death is but one
door of life closing and another opening to this same
world. Buddhists deny that the Ultimate Nothingness is
annihilation. But that seems out of touch with reality in
much the same way as the Hindu concept. The Buddhist
response is that I am failing to see reality properly. How
can I do that, then? By turning off my logic and mind
altogether. By not trying to make sense of things. This
amounts to "blind" faith—faith based on "nothing."

Most of the eastern religions have these same tenden-
cies, which is understandable since many of the eastern
religions have their roots in Hinduism and most of the
rest have been influenced by its philosophic ideas. Even
the modern New Age movement is rooted in Hinduism.

The Jewish Faith on Death

The Hebrew faith has a rich tradition dating back to the exodus from Egypt under the direction of the prophet, Moses. But over time it has undergone many changes. For example, today many Jews do not consider all Jewish Scripture to be of equal value. One author explains it this way:

> For us, the central part of the Five Books of Moses is the laws, described there as divinely revealed, which begin with the Ten Commandments in Exodus 20. What comes before, especially in Genesis, namely, the creation, the flood, Abraham, Isaac, and Jacob, and the enslavement and release in Egypt, constitutes materials which edify us or inspire us by motivating us to emulate personalities whose achievements we celebrate, such as Abraham and Moses. But the nub of our religion is to be obedient to the divinely revealed commandments which begin in Exodus 20. These provide us with our ceremonies and, beyond them, with our ethics.[18]

The Jewish canon has 39 books which are claimed as Scripture, and yet it is only those few chapters beginning in Exodus 20 that are considered to be truly "divinely revealed" and therefore worth paying close attention to and obeying.

What do the contemporary Jewish religionists believe today about things such as death, resurrection, and eternal living? Many Jews would ascribe to this belief:

> The Jewish view about obedience to the law can be put this way: Deliberate disobedience amounts to challenging God, and is unforgivable, and in time God, not man, will punish

such effrontery. Accidental, unwilled disobedience is forgivable, and divine forgiveness can be sought by man through repentance and through man's atonement; moreover, a man possesses the capacity to repent and to atone, and the free will to choose whether or not to conform to the laws, and then to do so.[19]

To be more specific, the teachers in Israel divided the law into 613 precepts. There were 365 negative ones and 248 positive ones. Even though Jews do not believe that the original sin of Adam and Eve had any bearing on man's sinfulness or ability to live rightly and please God, yet they do evidently believe that deliberate disobedience to any 613 precepts of the law is unforgivable. Only accidental sin is forgivable by God and atoneable by man. But their own Scriptures declare that every person has deliberately disobeyed God. King David himself declares:

> There is no one who does good. The Lord looks down from heaven on the sons of men to see if there are any who understand, any who seek God. All have turned aside, they have together become corrupt; there is no one who does good, not even one (Psalm 14:1-3. See also Isaiah 59:1-20).

And what about all the great heros of the Jewish faith? Every one of them deliberately disobeyed God, and this too is recorded in the Jewish Scriptures. Abraham deliberately lied about Sarah being his wife (Genesis 12:10-20). Moses deliberately rebelled against God's command and did not treat God as holy, but as common (Numbers 27:14). King David deliberately committed adultery with Bathsheba and then had her husband killed to cover his sin (2 Samuel 11:1-27).

This poses the question: Could anyone live an entire lifetime without deliberately disobeying just one of these laws?

Because of this paradox, and for many other reasons, many Jewish people today do not believe in life after death at all. One such testimony was shared by a Jewish man before his death:

> It is terrifying, but I feel it to be the truth, and we have no choice but to take advantage of the "accident" on one of the least of the planets and to live heroically, and to make the earth as livable as possible, and to cultivate, as long as we live, our sense of truth, justice, beauty, delicacy, and friendliness during the few years that are at our command. That's all we have at our disposal. And after that? There is no "after that," and there is no purpose, and we must learn not to fear the void that swallows us individually and in groups.[20]

Another Jewish writer expresses his ideas about death and beyond this way:

> Even within each of the three Jewish movements, there is the widest possible latitude for differences of opinion. There are many thoughts, yet none is declared authoritative and final. The tradition teaches, but, at the same time, seems to say there is much we do not know and still more we have to learn. ... Judaism's concern is more with life in the "here" than in the "hereafter," with this world's opportunities rather than with speculation about the world-to-come. Judaism helps its adherents of all ages to face death and to face away from it. It aids them to accept the reality

of death and protects them from destructive fantasy and illusion in the unconscious denial of fact. Most important of all, the Jewish religion offers an abundance of sharing religious resources in the encounter with helplessness, guilt, loneliness, and fear. Though reason cannot answer the why, and comforting words cannot wipe away tears, Judaism offers consolation in death by reaffirming life.[21]

Unfortunately, the bottom line is that Judaism is paradoxical and empty in the face of deeper issues such as death.

The Islamic Faith on Death

In A.D. 610 Ubu'l Kassim (Mohammed) began to have disturbing visions and revelations. Eventually he became convinced that Allah was the only true God, and that He was calling Mohammed to be His messenger.

In A.D. 622, nearly 600 years after the time of Christ, Mohammed made his historic flight from Mecca to Medina and officially began the religion known as Islam. Today Islam is an international religion with 17 percent of the world's population (mostly in Arab countries) claiming it as their faith.[22]

Mohammed traced the roots of Islam back to Abraham and Ishmael in Genesis 12-25.[23] He accepted the books of Moses, the Psalms, and the New Testament Gospels as part of the Islamic scripture. However, he considered them corrupt and so began to compile a more exact word from Allah. This was called the *Koran*. After Mohammed's death in A.D. 632 the *Koran* was finished by his disciples. It contains 114 chapters (called "surahs") and is shorter than the Christian New Testament. Mohammed believed Moses and Jesus were both great prophets of Allah,[24] but considered himself the greatest and last of the prophets.

Similarly to Christianity and historic Judaism, Islam believes in the resurrection of the dead. Reportedly speaking through Mohammed, Allah says:

> I swear by the Day of Resurrection, and by the self-reproaching soul! Does man think We shall never put his bones together again? Indeed, We can remold his very fingers! No, there shall be no escape. For on that day all shall return to Your Lord. On that day man shall be informed of all that he has done and all that he has failed to do. He shall become his own witness; his pleas shall go unheeded.... Does man think that he lives in vain? Was he not a drop of ejected semen? He became a clot of blood; then Allah formed and molded him and gave him male and female parts. Is He then not able to raise the dead to life?[25]

Islam also believes that one day Allah will allow heaven and earth, heaven and hell to pass away. One passage says that the time will come when the flames of hell will grow cold and it will turn green, such as in paradise.[26] There will be no *eternal* punishment. This teaching is unique to Islam.

But how does one attain heaven and avoid the temporary discomforts of hell? One writer answers this quite pointedly:

> Among the specific duties set forth in the quran [*Koran*] and spelled out in the traditions are the Five Pillars of Islam. These are five specific actions which a Muslim must perform in order to be saved. They are testimony of faith, prayer, almsgiving, fasting and the pilgrimage.[27]

In essence these are the five great "good deeds" one must do to attain heaven. In addition, participation in a holy war is also encouraged and rewarded.[28]

But how can one be sure he has done enough of these good works to merit paradise forever? Surah 101 of the *Koran*, titled "The Disaster," tells us:

> The Disaster! What is the Disaster?
> Would that you knew what the Disaster is!
> On that day men shall become like scattered moths and the mountains like tufts of corded wool.
> Then he whose scales are heavy shall dwell in bliss; but he whose scales are light, the Abyss shall be his home.
> Would that you knew what this is like!
> It is a scorching fire.[29]

When a person dies, their deeds will be weighed. If the good outweighs the bad, then they will go to heaven. If not, then they are bound for hell.

This raises some serious concerns. If a person cannot be sure his good deeds outweigh his bad before he dies, it is too late after he dies to do anything. Most people in the world have never made a pilgrimage to Mecca. Does that automatically mean they will go to hell? It does according to Islam. What about a God who does not give people the rules clearly, and yet sends them to a tormentous hell for not obeying? That is like spanking a child because he was not good enough today. How good is good enough? Who can possibly know?

✦ ✦ ✦

Even a brief overview of the world's great religions concerning the mysteries of death and dying is quite revealing. Adherents of Hinduism and Buddhism believe death is just the end of another stage of their continuing existence. A person climbs the spiritual ladder toward Ultimate Nothingness as he performs more and more good works (*karma*). Eventually, after enough life-times, he will be wholly good and at this stage become absorbed into the Universe (Ultimate Nothingness).

Judaism has mixed beliefs on death and dying. Many modern Jews do not believe in any form of life after death. They consider mankind to be animals, but believe we should be good and make the most of our dismal existence. Others of the Jewish faith who do believe in life after death say that if a person ever deliberately disobeys one of the 613 Jewish precepts, he cannot be forgiven.

Islam definitely believes all men die and all live eternally. Paradise is for those who, *after life is over*, tip the scales in favor of good works. Hell is for everyone else. But hell will eventually turn into paradise. This presents a fundamental problem. Nowhere in the *Koran* does Mohammed or Allah deal with the problem of sin as he sees it. There is a fundamental assumption that one good deed offsets one bad deed of equal weight. But no person can know how he fares until it is too late to do anything about it.

Neither Judaism nor Islam has an answer for the question: "How good is good enough?" Even if goodness *were* the key to life after death, how can anyone determine the qualitative and quantitative correlates of "goodness"? If I assume God or Allah is the measure of what is ultimately "good," then who measures up? And if God or Allah accepts less than 100 percent from mankind, then they are gods who compromise what they themselves say is "good," and that is "not good" to Jew or Muslim. Judaism and Islam appear to be more reasonable and rational than Hinduism or Buddhism in their attempts to deal with God and death, but they end up being empty religions when it comes to giving real answers to the deep questions about life and death.

Christianity is different from every other religion in the world. The gospel of Christ is the gospel of grace, not based on anything we can do in our own strength but rather on what Jesus has already done through his death on the cross. Christianity offers us an evidential hope for real life, an abundant fullness of life, both in the present, and for all eternity. And after all, isn't that what we need when our lives have been changed forever by the death of someone near?

Notes

Chapter 3—The Agony of Empty Arms

1. James M. Sinacore, "Avoiding the Humanistic Aspect of Death: An Outcome from the Implicit Elements of Health Professions Education," *Death Education* 5 (Summer 1981), p. 130.
2. Avery D. Weisman, *On Dying and Denying* (New York: Behavioral Publications, 1972), p. 8.
3. Ibid., p. 213.

Chapter 4—The Raging of a Tormented Soul

1. Larry Richards and Paul Johnson, *Death and the Caring Community: Ministering to the Terminally Ill* (Portland, OR: Multnomah, 1980)., pp. 29-30.
2. Ibid., p. 37.
3. Michael Simpson, *The Facts of Death* (Englewood Cliffs, NJ: Prentice Hall, 1979), p. 48.

Chapter 5—Why Can't I Rejoice?

1. Lily Pincus, *Death and the Family* (New York: Pantheon Books, 1974), p. 13.

Chapter 6—The Battle to Get Back to Normal

1. C.S. Lewis, *A Grief Observed* (England: Faber and Faber, 1961; reprint ed., New York: Bantam Books, 1980), pp. 10-11.
2. E. Millay, "Renascence ii," *Collected Sonnets* (New York: Harper and Row, 1946), p. 2.

Chapter 8—Facts and Fictions

1. Interview with Woody Allen, *Time*, April 30, 1979.
2. Weisman, *On Dying and Denying*, p. 8.
3. Jacques Choron, *Suicide* (New York: Charles Scribner's Sons, 1972), p. 60.

Chapter 10—Why Did He Have to Die?

1. C.S. Lewis, *Mere Christianity* (New York, Macmillan, 1943), pp. 55-56.

Chapter 14—Loving Again

1. C.S. Lewis, *The Four Loves* (New York: A Harvest/HJB Book, 1960), p. 169.

Appendix A—Is There Really a Loving God?

1. Lehman Strauss, *When Loved Ones Are Taken in Death* (Grand Rapids: Zondervan, 1964), p. 5.

Appendix B—Empty Religions

1. Lewis Browne, *The World's Great Scriptures* (New York: Macmillan, 1961), p. 66.
2. Ibid., p. 76.
3. Ibid., pp. 125-126.
4. Ibid., p. 84.
5. Ibid., p. 88.
6. Ibid., pp. 110-111.
7. Ibid., p. 84.
8. Jose Pereira, *Hindu Theology: A Reader* (New York: Image Books, 1976), p. 355.
9. George N. Marshall, *Buddha: The Quest for Serenity* (Boston: Beacon Press, 1978), p. 54.

10. Ibid., p. 40.
11. Ibid., p. 41.
12. Kenneth Boa, *Cults, World Religions and You* (Wheaton, IL: Victor Books, 1977), p. 27.
13. Browne, *The World's Great Scripture*, p. 134.
14. Ibid., pp. 166-167.
15. Ibid., pp. 167-169.
16. Ibid., p. 199.
17. Ibid., p. 200.
18. Samuel Sandmel, *We Jews and You Christians* (New York: J.P. Lippencott, 1967), pp. 67-68.
19. Ibid., p. 69.
20. Jack Riemer, ed., *Jewish Reflections on Death* (New York: Schocker, 1974), p. 148.
21. Earl A. Grollman, ed., "The Ritualistic and Theological Approach of the Jews," *Explaining Death to Children* (Boston: Beacon Press, 1967), pp. 237, 242.
22. David B. Barrett, ed., *World Christian Encyclopedia* (New York: Oxford University Press, 1982), pp. 4-7.
23. *The Holy Koran: An Introduction with Selections*, A.J. Arberry, trans. and ed. (New York: Macmillan, 1953), p. 93.
24. Ibid., pp. 126-131.
25. Bertrand Russell, *Why I Am Not a Christian* (New York: Simon and Schuster, 1957), pp. 55-56.
26. Frithjof Schuon, *Dimensions of Islam*, P.N. Townsend, trans. (London: George Allen and Unwin Ltd., 1970), pp. 136-137.
27. John Sabini, *Islam: A Primer* (Washington, D.C., Middle East Editorial Associated, n.d.), p. 16.
28. *The Holy Koran*, Arberry, p. 137.
29. *The Koran*, N.J. Dawood, trans. and ed., 4th ed. (New York: Penguin Books, 1974), p. 29.

Recommended Reading

Bayly, Joseph. *The View from a Hearse*. Elgin, IL: David C. Cook, 1973.

Bluebond-Langner, Myra. *The Private World of Dying Children*. Princeton, NJ: Princeton University Press, 1978.

Geisler, Norman L. *The Roots of Evil*. Response by John W. Wenham. Grand Rapids: Zondervan Publishing House, 1978.

Kopp, Ruth. *Where Has Grandpa Gone?* Grand Rapids: Zondervan, 1983.

Lewis, C.S. *A Grief Observed*. England: Faber and Faber Limited, 1961; reprint ed., New York: Bantam Books, 1980.

_____. *The Problem of Pain*. New York: Macmillan, 1962.

Richards, Larry, and Johnson, Paul. *Death and the Caring Community: Ministering to the Terminally Ill*. Portland, OR: Multnomah Press, 1980.

Simpson, Michael A. *The Facts of Death*. Englewood Cliffs, NJ: Prentice Hall, 1979.

Swindoll, Charles. *For Those Who Hurt*. Portland, OR: Multnomah Press, 1977.

Taylor, Patrick L. "Searching for God in Death." D.Min. diss., Dallas Theological Seminary, 1985.